After You,
Mark Twain

Be good + you will be lonesome.

Mark Twain

After You, Mark Twain

A Modern Journey Around the Equator

Betty Wetzel

Fulcrum Publishing
Golden, Colorado

Copyright © 1990
Betty Wetzel

Book Design by
Jody Chapel, Cover to Cover Design

Photographs courtesy of the Mark Twain Project, Main Library,
University of California, Berkeley

Line illustrations taken from *Following the Equator: A Journey
Around the World*, by Mark Twain, The American Publishing
Company (Hartford, Conn.: 1897), first edition.

Library of Congress Cataloging-in-Publication Data

Wetzel, Betty.
    After you, Mark Twain : a modern journey around the equator /
Betty Wetzel.
      p.   cm.
    ISBN 1-55591-069-6
    1. Twain, Mark, 1835–1910--Journeys. 2. Twain, Mark, 1835-
1910. Following the equator. 3. Authors, American--19th century-
-Journeys. 4. Voyages around the world. 5. Wetzel, Betty--Journeys.
I. Title.
PS1334.W48   1990
818'.409--dc20
[B]   90-37972
                                          CIP

Printed in the United States of America

10 9 8 7 6 5 4 3 2 1

Fulcrum Publishing
350 Indiana Street
Golden, Colorado 80401

For Winston, who went with me all the way

Contents

"Travel is fatal to prejudice, bigotry, and narrowmindedness, and many of our people need it sorely on these accounts. Broad, wholesome, charitable views of men and things cannot be acquired by vegetating in one little corner of the earth all one's lifetime."
—Mark Twain, *The Innocents Abroad*

CHAPTER I

Introduction

> A lazy man doesn't rush around with his
> notebook as soon as he lands on a foreign shore. He
> simply drifts about, and if anything gets in his way
> of sufficient interest to make an impression on him,
> it goes into his book. ... What's the use of making a
> business of travelling when you are out for pleasure?
> Mark Twain Interview
> *Portland Oregonian*
> August 10, 1895

I first read *Following the Equator* in the "authorized
uniform edition" of Mark Twain's complete works,
bound in dark green and shelved in a glass-fronted
bookcase in my family living room in Roundup, Montana.
My father, editor and publisher of the weekly newspaper,
the *Roundup Record*, was a Twain devotee. Over the
years the volumes *Tom Sawyer* and *The Adventures of
Huckleberry Finn* became dog-eared, but I think I was the
only member of the household who read the two-volume
book, *Following the Equator*. I made up my mind then
that some day I would travel to those places and see those
fascinating lands.

My husband, Winston, had the same yen to see those
places, but his curiosity had been piqued by a quite
different source. The son of an evangelical minister in
Minnesota, he had spent rainy afternoons of his boyhood

AFTER YOU, MARK TWAIN

perusing *The Earth Girdled, The World as Seen To-day* ("magnificently illustrated with 400 photographic views"), by the Reverend T. DeWitt Talmage, D.D. Mark Twain and the Reverend Dr. Talmage had travelled similar routes, with the latter concentrating on visiting foreign missions, a subject of frequent ridicule by Samuel L. Clemens.

Over the years of a long marriage, we often talked of the faraway places of our childhood imaginings inspired by the two voyages. Now Winston, a retired public school superintendent, and I, a compulsive journalist, were pushing seventy. Our four children were grown and married. We had been *around* the world almost twenty years earlier when Winston was posted as an education advisor for a University of Chicago project in Dacca, East Pakistan (now Dhaka, Bangladesh). But we had not *seen* the world.

Certainly our earlier experience was an advantage, for we understood the basic mechanics of foreign travel. We were sure that we would be equal to it. Perhaps adventure was in our genes and in our blood, for our ancestors had crossed the continent in covered wagons. This was our chance for some twentieth-century pioneering. But we deplore aimless wandering. We didn't want to go as tourists, but as travellers. We wanted to go on our own. Why hire a tour guide to protect us from the natives? What we needed was some objective, some destination, some purpose for our journey.

It occurred to me to follow Mark Twain's 1895–96 lecture tour to the British colonies. We could visit the countries he described in *Following the Equator* and I would write a book telling of our adventures. Perhaps it would be possible to find some evidence of his visit— newspaper interviews, reviews of his lectures. Almost a century had passed since his voyage, and the changes

2

INTRODUCTION

wrought by industrialization and the dissolution of the British Empire should be worth reporting.

Winston fell in with my suggestion. We took turns reading *Following the Equator* and laid out our itinerary: Hawaii, Fiji, New Zealand, Australia, Thailand, India, Sri Lanka, and South Africa. Our loft became littered with maps, old copies of *National Geographic*, travel books, opened encylopedias, brochures from travel agencies, atlases, newspaper clippings. We concluded that the best plan would be to buy round-the-world air tickets, and make our own arrangements once we landed at each destination.

Preparations took a year. Our passports had expired. Visas would be needed. Immunizations were required or recommended for everything but smallpox, now eradicated. We had to make the two-hundred-mile trip to Missoula twice for the cholera and yellow fever shots needed for travel in India and South Africa. A precautionary first aid kit against such frailties as blisters, fever, and diarrhea was a necessity. We both made lists—clothes for several climates, rain gear, and, most important of all, comfortable (but respectable) shoes. We couldn't forget our tennis rackets and cribbage board. And we had to find a home for Benji, our golden retriever.

In retrospect, it was fortunate that we undertook our grand adventure when we did. Since we returned, uprisings and revolutions and wars and tidal waves have afflicted the countries we visited, and we are frequently horrified and saddened by the nightly news.

It took us a little more than four months to retrace Mark Twain's voyage, which had lasted a year. Our travel was mostly by jet and was not interrupted by appearances on the lecture platform. Then, too, Twain was met at dockside by British officialdom and entertained at lavish parties by reigning nawabs and princes. Our arrivals

3

were noted only by customs agents. Oddly, few people we met on our journey were aware that Mark Twain had ever visited their countries. Except for a few excerpts in anthologies, *Following the Equator*, published in Britain under the title *More Tramps Abroad*, is almost unknown today.

Twain warmed up for his 1895 lecture tour with twenty-one appearances in the northern tier of states en route to his port of departure, Vancouver, British Columbia. After a shaky start in midwestern towns from Cleveland to Crookston, Minnesota, he hit his stride in Butte, Montana. Major J.B. Pond, manager of his stateside tour, reported: "I found myself listening, and sat through the lecture, enjoying every word. It actually seemed as if I had never known him to be quite so good. The house was full and very responsive."

It took Mark Twain forty days to lecture his way by rail across the continent that summer of 1895. Finally arriving in Victoria, the party learned that smoke from raging forest fires had prevented their steamer, the *Warrimoo*, from docking. Repairs took another week, but what's a week's delay on a year's sea voyage? The crossing from Victoria to Hawaii took seven days.

Mark Twain was afflicted with carbuncles when he started his journey. In debt to the tune of $100,000, he hoped that his lecture tour to the English-speaking colonies and his subsequent book would make him solvent. Today his carbuncles would have been cured by an antibiotic, his debt would have been in the millions, and jet travel would have quartered the time. Accompanying him on the voyage were his wife, his daughter Clara, his manager, sixteen pieces of hand luggage, and several steamer trunks. Travel was not lightly undertaken by women in those days of oversized hats, corsets, bustles, voluminous skirts, and petticoats. Twain, who lectured in

INTRODUCTION

formal wear, wore only white in the tropics, including dress suits of white cashmere.

Before sailing he made an announcement: "I intend the lectures as well as the property for the creditors. ... I am confident that if I live I can pay the last debt within four years, after which, at the age of 64, I can make a fresh and unencumbered start in life." At the end of 1898, with all debts paid, he had $107,000 in the bank. To celebrate he bought a box of six-cent cigars, instead of the four-and-a-half centers he usually smoked.

We were not encumbered by debts or steamer trunks. As we left our home on Flathead Lake in western Montana on November 18, 1983, our luggage consisted of one suitcase apiece and a carry-on bag. It was barely dawn, but the shoreline of the lake and the snowy crags of the Mission Mountains could be made out. I gulped a breath of piney air, took a long look at the lake, and got into the car for the thirty-two-mile drive to Glacier International Airport near Kalispell, the first leg of our journey of some thirty-five thousand miles to circle the planet.

Western Montana is one of the most isolated and faraway places in the lower forty-eight. There is no such thing as a direct flight to Seattle, Denver, Minneapolis, or Calgary. If you live in this corner of northwest Montana you have to "crow hop" over the mountains on obscure carriers and catch a connecting flight to somewhere better connected with the outside world. We were bound for Los Angeles via Spokane and Salt Lake City, a journey that took the better part of the day and entailed a two-hour layover watching enormous Mormon families congregating for the coming Thanksgiving holiday. The home of our eldest daughter in Dana Point, California, was where we savored the last sensation of home and family before we began to follow Mark Twain around the equator.

CHAPTER II

Paradise Isles

> If I could have my way about it, I would go
> back there and remain the rest of my days. It is
> paradise for an indolent man. If a man is rich he can
> live expensively, and his grandeur will be respected
> as in other parts of the earth; if he is poor he can
> herd with the natives and live on next to nothing.
>
> Mark Twain
> *Sacramento Union*, 1866

Hawaii, where Mark Twain had spent several months in 1866 as a reporter for the *Sacramento Union*, was to be the first engagement of his lecture tour. He wrote: "On the seventh day out we saw a dim vast bulk standing up out of the wastes of the Pacific and knew that that spectral promontory was Diamond Head, a piece of this world which I had not seen before for twenty-nine years. So we were nearing Honolulu, the capital city of the Sandwich Islands—those islands which to me were Paradise; a Paradise which I had been longing all those years to see again. Not any other thing in the world could have stirred me as the sight of that great rock did."

Then came word that cholera had broken out. Honolulu was quarantined. More than sixteen hundred dollars had to be refunded to the sold-out house. It was an inauspicious beginning for his lecture tour. Although the

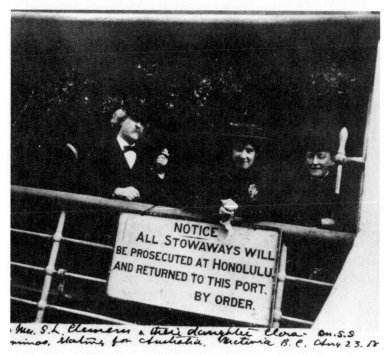

Mr. S.L. Clemens & their daughter Clara - On S.S minos. starting for Australia. Victoria B.C. Aug 23. 18

epidemic prevented Mark Twain from revisiting the Sandwich Islands, it was on his itinerary. Like him, we had been there before, but we saw no reason not to pause here again. The flight from Los Angeles to Hawaii is long enough to justify a rest stop.

It is disconcerting to fly more than two thousand miles across the Pacific Ocean and land in the United States. At first blush it looked like Hawaii, all right—palm trees and hibiscus and gentle rain, then, before we could get to our hotel, cottony clouds appearing as though hung out by stagehands. Suddenly the sky was blue, the sun was hot, and the moisture in the air confirmed that we were in the tropics. We could almost feel our skin smoothing and our hair beginning to curl.

AFTER YOU, MARK TWAIN

But the highrise hotels, office buildings and department stores on the beach at Waikiki seemed singularly inappropriate for the proper practice of indolence. We passed them by. One of our objectives was not to "herd" with tourists, at least American tourists. We herded instead with the Japanese. The Makaha, a sprawling, artfully designed hideout at the tip of Oahu island, was beautiful and unlike the Hiltons and Holiday Inns of Honolulu. It had the flavor of the orient, or at least of Japan. Both shower and toilet bore Japanese instructions. On the bedside table, alongside the Gideon Bible, was *The Teachings of Buddha.* Japanese couples deferred to our white hair in the breakfast line, on the tennis courts, and going in and out of doors, bowing and smiling whenever we met. We found it pleasant. Back home we were not accustomed to deference.

Our Hawaiian bus driver, with whom we became well acquainted on the long drives to Makaha, distrusted the Japanese. He had watched the attack on Pearl Harbor when he was eight years old. "Then a few years ago, I saw Japanese planes over the harbor dropping bombs and I said, 'Oh, no, not again!' Then I found out that they were only filming *Tora! Tora! Tora!* They bombed us with bombs in 1942. Today they're bombing us with money."

Hawaii is becoming more and more "Japanized." Its three-term governor, George Ariyoshi, was the son of a sumo wrestler who migrated from Japan in 1926. With the continuing influx of Americans from the mainland, the population is becoming increasingly *haole* (white), and is further diluted by more than four million sun-seekers who come each year to join the 800,000 regular residents. Only seven of the fifty-one members of Hawaii's House of Representatives are Hawaiians; only three of twenty-five senators. So what is Hawaii? A Japanized, Americanized melting pot? We had only a few days to find out.

PARADISE ISLES

It's not easy to find "real" Hawaiians. When Captain James Cook reached the islands in 1778, there were probably about 300,000 natives. By the time Mark Twain was there in 1866, disease brought by western sailors had cut their population to about seventy thousand. The 1980 census listed only some ninety-five hundred full-blooded Hawaiians. We discovered Hawaiians on the "Bus," which carries you anywhere on Oahu for fifty cents. It was transportation for the poor, the aged, working people, students, and us.

Eyes—not slanted, but set somewhat at an angle, wide apart and almond-shaped, the whites bone-white and glistening—were to us the most compelling feature of Hawaiians. People watched us openly and with interest. Other races may also have dark skins and black hair, but Hawaiian eyes are somehow spellbinding and beautiful. In contrast to the Japanese, few wore glasses. Listening to Hawaiian people talk is like hearing music, and no wonder. Their language has only twelve letters—*h*, *k*, *l*, *m*, *n*, *p*, *w*, *a*, *e*, *i*, *o*, *u*—and every word ends in a vowel.

Friendly but disgruntled young Hawaiian men complained to Winston that they must leave the islands to find anything but service or laboring jobs connected with tourism, the sugar industry, and the military base. Education beyond high school seems pointless, as well as being beyond their means. A beautiful old woman of Chinese-Hawaiian-English descent apologized to me for the rowdy behavior of some schoolchildren. (I hadn't noticed.) "Discipline is out of fashion," she observed. Mother of seven children, she was returning from her job as a gardener. As she left the bus she pointed out her shanty on a beach lot for which she paid one dollar a year rent to the government. It was light years away from the Waikiki Hilton.

We could see the results of the delicious Hawaiian

foods in the girth of many older Hawaiians. The *kalua* pork, poi, and coconut pudding showed particularly in ample older women in *mu-mus*, with their hair in topknots like Bloody Mary's. In this hot climate they did, however, look much more comfortable than the American woman we followed on the street with her peach-colored polyester shorts stretched to their full tensile strength.

We took the Bus to witness the Duke Kahanamoka Surfing Classic scheduled for the Banzai Pipeline on the north shore of Oahu. Riding completely inside the curl of those ferocious waves is said to be the ultimate surfing experience. The event was to be televised by NBC "Sportsworld." When we arrived at the site we learned that the waves were so wild and dangerous that the contest had been cancelled. However, that didn't stop the contestants who were out warming up for the event.

We talked to one of these bronzed nomads as he flushed sand from himself and his board under an outdoor shower. A North Carolina college dropout, he'd been here for three years, herding with the natives and sharing a shack with a friend for fifty dollars a month.

We asked about a surfer's life. "Well," he said, "You get up in the morning and look at the surf and then decide how to spend the day."

Winston asked, "What do your parents think about this?"

"Not much," he grinned.

As a reporter Mark Twain had suggested that the United States annex the Sandwich Islands and make of them "a fine half-way house for our Pacific-plying ships." He also pointed out the advantages to owning Kilauea, "the mightiest volcano on earth," which could be run by Barnum. By annexing the Hawaiians "we can afflict them with our wise and beneficent government. ... We can make that little bunch of sleepy islands the hottest corner on earth, and array it in the moral splendor of our high and holy civilization."

On July 7, 1898, Hawaii was annexed to the United States. It became the fiftieth state in 1959. Today there is a movement to redefine a Hawaiian as any person who can prove that an ancestor could have been on the beach to meet Captain Cook when he landed on Hawaii in 1778. Intermarriage has made this proof difficult, but it is a question that matters since it determines whether or not people are eligible to claim land under the Hawaiian Homes Act and to gain admission to the exclusive Kamehameha School, reserved for children of Hawaiian descent.

A small radical group wants to secede from the United States. On a dumpster on the beach we saw scrawled: "The Nation of Hawaii." There's a movement to revive native identity. The state constitution requires public schools to offer courses in the Hawaiian language, culture, and history. There is growing interest in learning the proper performance of ancient hula.

Hawaii's reputation as a place to retire or a place to play, rather than a place to do business, makes its economic future bleak. Even tourism is not assured forever. By the year 2000, water is going to be a luxury in Hawaii. The rainfall which replenishes the lens-shaped aquifer under-lying Oahu is not up to the prodigious bathroom habits of the growing numbers of sun-seekers and retirees. They may bring money to the islands, but they don't furnish their own water. Increasing salt content in underground reserves and pesticide contamination compound the problem.

We didn't take surfing lessons, ride an outrigger canoe, learn hula, or take up the ukulele. We didn't buy a T-shirt inscribed "I Got Lei'd in Hawaii." Nor did we grapple with the Hawaiian language, which seemed fraught with possibilities for error. For instance, the word *lua* means hole in the ground or toilet, while *lu'au*, as every tourist knows, means feast. We were told that the mountains of Hawaii, when measured from the bottom of the ocean floor, are higher than Everest.

* * *

Sailors have the leisure to savor the approach to and crossing of the earth's coordinates. For jet travellers cartography simply presents a logistical puzzle in the adjustment of digital watches. While punching tiny buttons to realign the time, date, and day of the week, we missed both the equator and the international date line on our night flight from Honolulu to Nadi in Fiji.

Not so Mark Twain, who made much of both. "Crossed the equator. In the distance it looked like a blue ribbon stretched across the ocean. Several passengers kodak'd it." As for the date line: "Tomorrow we shall be close to the center of the globe. ... And then we must lose a day out of our lives, a day never to be found again. We shall all die one day earlier than from the beginning of time we were foreordained to die. We shall be a day behindhand all through eternity." And after he had crossed it, he reflected upon it further.

> Sure enough, it has happened. Yesterday it was September 8, Sunday; today, it is September 10, Tuesday. There is something uncanny about it. And uncomfortable. ...
> If the ships all moved in the one direction—westward, I mean—the world would suffer a prodigious loss in the matter of valuable time, through the dumping overboard on the Great Meridian of such multitudes of days by ships' crews and passengers. But, fortunately, the ships do not all sail

west, half of them sail east. ... These latter pick up
all the discarded days and add them to the world's
stock again; and about as good as new, too; for of
course the salt water preserves them.

"CROSSING THE EQUATOR"

AFTER YOU, MARK TWAIN

The *Fiji Times* (established 1869) also makes much of this. Beneath its name is the arresting epigram: "The First Newspaper Published in the World Today," followed by the explanation, "Suva [the capital city] is just west of the International Date Line where the new day begins." It is a refreshing and novel idea.

The newest day in the whole world was just dawning. We drove from the airport at Nadi (pronounced *Nandi*) into a luminous pink mist which lingered on the long drive across the island. Smoke from breakfast fires curled from thatched huts. Small boys drove family cows in for milking. There was a yawning sense of the awakening day across the rural landscape.

In contrast to the highrises of Waikiki, the Fijian Resort Hotel on Yanuca Island was a sprawling complex on the beach with no roofline higher than the tallest palm. Started by Pan American and Air Quantas pilots for their personal rest and recreation after World War II, the hotel claimed to be "quite simply, one of the best resorts in the world." It was apparent that those pilots had had their pick of islands.

Gradually their little hideaway grew to 80 and then to its present 316 rooms. The dining room opened on ocean and swimming pool. Footpaths meandered past exotic shrubs and artfully placed tropical flowers. A small army of gardeners moved about gathering dropped leaves and palm fronds, and plucking faded hibiscus blooms. Hidden from view but handy were tennis courts and a golf course. From the swimming pool we could hear "Jingle Bells," "White Christmas," and "Joy to the World" in Fijian. Strings of colored lights entwined in palm trees did little to convince us that Christmas was coming.

Watching over it all was Patema, the doorman of the Fijian since the landing of the first pilots. Ample of height and girth, he wore a navy blue wraparound skirt *(sulu)* banded in pale blue, the effect of which was amazingly masculine, not to say seductive. So was the single frangipani flower in his hair.

"This must have been a great party place in the old days," I observed.

He showed a fine row of white teeth and chuckled, "You got it."

It was Patema who told me that the Fijian had been acquired by a Singapore–Malaysian hotel chain, which planned further expansion. Patema and the similarly garbed bellhops, all heavily built with immense calves and triple-E-wide feet, epitomized our western notion of South Sea islanders. Mark Twain described them: "Handsome, great dusky men they were, muscular, clean-limbed, and with faces full of character and intelligence," and the women, "tall, straight, comely, nobly built, sweeping by with chin up, and a gait incomparable for unconscious stateliness and dignity."

Their government apparently wishes to protect them from corruption by foreigners. Before landing in Nadi, we had been handed the following warning: "Holders of visitors' permits must not while in Fiji: (1) Behave in a manner prejudicial to peace and good order; (2) Engage in: (a) any business, profession or employment whether for reward or not; (b) religious vocation; (c) research; except with the approval of the Permanent Secretary for Labour, Industrial Relations and Immigration."

We did not, while in Fiji, prejudice the island's peace and good order, and we did not intend to become involved in research or religious vocation. It just happened. It was the fault of a headline in the *Get-About Guide*, compliments of the Fiji Beach Press. VISIT THE MUSEUM it ordered in bold type. So we took the Coral Coach Express of Fiji, Ltd., an ancient Leyland bus, to Suva.

The museum was located in Thurston Gardens, next

to Government House. We ran for it through a tropical downpour and spent the whole afternoon there. Winston was enchanted with a 118-foot outrigger canoe called the Drua. Built for a great chief, using the most primitive tools and fiber sails, its oars, thirty-two feet long, were hewn from a single tree.

In an obscure corner of the museum I discovered, mounted on the wall behind glass, all that had been found of Thomas Baker, a Methodist missionary killed and eaten by Fijians in 1867—the soles of his shoes, a few coins, and a piece of soap. Nearby was the pot in which he had been cooked, the wooden plate on which he had been served, and the fork with which he had been eaten. There was a letter to his wife describing the "heathenism" which he was shortly to attack: "One's heart aches at the recollection that there in the mountains are to be found savages as wild, as wicked, as naked as any who have yet been met with on the coast. ... We hope ere long all will bow the knee and own Jesus as Lord."

Fergus Clunie, the handsome, bearded young curator of the museum, answered our questions about the incident and pointed out that Mr. Baker was the *only* missionary to have been eaten by the Fijians and that, in fact, he had been executed for cause in the light of Fiji custom and practice.

The Reverend Mr. Baker had made arrangements with Nauluwavu, the chief of the village of Navuso, to hold a missionary meeting with his tribe. Nauluwavu, pleased and honored, extended the invitation to his people and made the necessary preparations. Without consulting Nauluwavu, Mr. Baker then changed his mind and held the meeting at Rewa, a neighboring village.

Upon learning of this insult, Nauluwavu put out a contract on the missionary by sending a whale's tooth to a friendly neighboring tribe, asking them to kill the missionary. This was the custom. By accepting the whale's tooth, that tribe would undertake to do the wishes of the giver. It was an inviolable agreement.

Realizing that the missionary was an important and holy man, the first tribe declined and the whale tooth was passed from tribe to tribe until at last it was accepted by Nawabalavu, a chief who had never seen Baker and had no grudge against him. According to an eyewitness, after an ambush, the Fijians ate everything but a piece of soap "which they thought was a piece of bread made from bananas, but finding it bitter, they threw it away and his money, too."

The museum received the cooking pot and serving utensils many years later, together with a letter from the tribe. They were brought to a successor of Mr. Baker's in the Methodist mission by a descendant of Chief Nauluwavu, in an attempt to break the evil spell which had befallen the tribe. Since having the missionary killed, they had been decimated by disease, defeat, and ill fortune. It was their belief that by presenting the implements of the feast to Mr. Baker's successor, they might earn forgiveness and an end to their bad luck. Contrary to popular cartoons, missionaries are not cooked in black pots, such as were used by our pioneer ancestors to make soap or render lard. At least in Fiji, they were steamed in clay vessels.

Mark Twain makes no mention of the Reverend Mr. Baker, although the incident had happened only twenty-seven years earlier. But then Twain took a dim view of missionaries: "Extending the Blessings of Civilization to our Brother who Sits in Darkness has been a good trade and has paid well, on the whole; and there is money in it yet, if carefully worked—but not enough, in my judgment, to make any considerable risk advisable. The People that Sit in Darkness are getting to be too scarce—too scarce and too shy." Nevertheless, today most Fijians are Christians—primarily Methodists.

Cyclone Oscar, one of the 1983 "El Nino" hurricanes, had hit Fiji the February before we got there. (A tropical cyclone is a storm equivalent to a typhoon or a hurricane.) Ragged trees, damaged roofs, and eroded beaches were still in evidence. Hurricanes appear to be more of a threat to travellers in the South Pacific than disease or terrorists. Fiji is today malaria free and as healthy a tropical island as can be found. It has much to recommend it. It's about as close as you can conveniently come to standing on the equator. In December it was comfortably hot, but blessedly cooled by afternoon showers. The year-round temperature averages seventy-two, seldom falling below seventy or rising above ninety degrees.

A CYCLONE

PARADISE ISLES

Although 40 percent of the population is Indian—primarily Hindus, originally imported by British planters as laborers on sugar estates—these people are kept out of sight of travellers. Fijians in native costume staff hotel desks, travel agencies, and airline ticket offices, and sing and dance for tourists. But we learned from reading the *Fiji Times* that behind the scenes Indians dominate business and the professions, keep the books, and run the shops. Fijians, however, have managed to keep political control by adroitly instituting a three-house parliament divided into Fijians, Indians, and Europeans. Power rests almost totally in the hands of the Fijian assembly. Indians aren't allowed to own land. I asked an elderly British colonial if Fijians and Indians intermarry. The answer: "Seldom. Nor do the Fijians marry whites."

Fiji is not a prosperous country, but it feeds its own people with homegrown rice, taro, yams, fruits, and vegetables. It exports sugar cane, coconuts, and bananas. What Fiji needs is a cash crop of tourist dollars. But how many people can find Fiji on a map? We couldn't have before we went there. To make the country known to other than crossword puzzle fans, the Fiji Chamber of Commerce could begin by designing a logo around a single shared dot for the last three letters of its name. Then follow up with a television special showing Captain William Bligh blown by the trade winds through the islands after the *Bounty* mutiny.

Money for the development of first class tourist accommodations is being sought by the Fiji Tourist Board, while right before their eyes in the capital city of Suva stands the Grand Pacific Hotel. Beautifully landscaped and strategically located on the main thoroughfare between Government House and the ocean, it was built at the turn of the century by the Union Steam Ship Company for

Pacific-plying passengers. Its "colonial" wing is designed like first class shipboard cabins. Each room opens onto a shaded balcony to catch the cooling trade winds and on the opposite side another balcony overlooks the lobby, which rises three stories to banks of ceiling fans and stained-glass windows.

"A magnificent structure," the *Fiji Times* proclaimed at its opening, "its lavatory accommodations are the most lavish and sanitary as modern science can make them... No less than 11 Twyford's cast iron enamelled baths are provided." And—the epitome of luxury—storage tanks on the roof featured movable lids so that bath water might be iced.

The Grand Pacific Hotel is today seedy and well populated by cockroaches. The dining room is closed, as are the public rooms. Four young Australian backpackers, two Indians making a business deal, and a bearded old salt who looked like Ernest Hemingway were the only occupants of the fan-backed wicker chairs in the lobby. But there's nothing wrong with the Grand Pacific Hotel that a good cleaning, modern plumbing, air conditioning, and an exterminator couldn't fix. It has all the charm and spaciousness to which ladies and gentlemen travelling by steamship were accustomed. If it were properly run, American tourists would love it.

When these islands became a possession and dependency of the British crown in 1874, native Fijians, of mixed Melanesian and Polynesian blood, made up almost the entire population. A British tourist of the time wrote that the amount of gin consumed by white traders and sailors tippling in the public saloons was amazing, while simultaneously British Wesleyan and French Catholic missionaries competed for souls. In the next fifty years the native population fell from 200,000 to 83,000, by

which time Fijians were outnumbered by foreigners—
Indians, Europeans, Chinese, and people from other islands. The Fijians became a minority in their own country. After being a colony for ninety-six years, Fiji became
an independent member of the British Commonwealth of
Nations on October 10, 1970, and has since asserted itself
accordingly. It was in Fiji that we first read of the concern
of Pacific island countries about the dumping of low-level
nuclear waste in the ocean.

SOUTHERN CROSS

Looking up in the vel-
vety darkness of a night on
Fiji, we noticed a problem
with the sky of the southern
hemisphere. As visitors we
found it not only unsatis-
factory but disorienting.
With no Big Dipper, no
Orion, no North Star, the
heavens seemed featureless
and confused. While there
was no shortage of stars,
they were scattered about
with no apparent pattern.
We had expected to get our
bearings from the Southern Cross which, we assumed,
would direct us to the South Star. It was shocking to
discover that there is no South Star. And as for the
Southern Cross—we couldn't even find it. We were to
search for it in vain in Fiji, New Zealand, Australia, and
South Africa. Mark Twain had similar problems:

> Yesterday evening we saw the Big Dipper and
> the north star sink below the horizon and disappear
> from our world. ... It is no matter. I am tired of them
> anyway. I think they are well enough, but one doesn't
> want them always hanging around. My interest was

AFTER YOU, MARK TWAIN

all in the Southern Cross. I had never seen that. I had heard about it all my life, and it was but natural that I should be burning to see it. No other constellation makes so much talk. I had nothing against the Big Dipper—and naturally couldn't have anything against it, since it is a citizen of our own sky, and the property of the United States—but I did want it to move out of the way and give this foreigner a chance. Judging by the size of the talk which the Southern Cross had made, I supposed it would need a sky all to itself.

But that was a mistake. We saw the Cross tonight, and it was not large. Not large, and not strikingly bright. But it was low down toward the horizon, and it may improve when it gets up higher in the sky. It is ingeniously named, for it looks just as a cross would look if it looked like something else. But that description does not describe; it is too vague, too general, too indefinite. It does after a fashion suggest a cross—a cross that is out of repair— or out of drawing; not correctly shaped. It is long, with a short cross-bar, and the cross-bar is canted out of the straight line.

MARK TWAIN WAITING AT DOCKSIDE

22

CHAPTER III

Junior England
New Zealand

> If it would not look too much like showing off,
> I would tell the reader where New Zealand is; for he
> is as I was: he thinks he knows ... people think that
> New Zealand is close to Australia or Asia ... and that
> you cross to it on a bridge. But that is not so. It is not
> close to anything, but lies by itself, out in the water.
>
> Mark Twain

New Zealand stretches for eleven hundred miles midway between the equator and the South Pole. No spot in the two skinny islands which make it up is further than seventy miles from the sea. Whatever climate is preferred can be found somewhere on one of these islands. Both islands combined are about the size of California and slightly smaller than Japan.

To explore the country we rented a car, until we noticed that driving and looking were incompatible. Thenceforth, we left the driving to the locals, who are accustomed to driving on the wrong side of the road, and know where they're going. We enrolled briefly in a minibus tour (the driver was called a courier), and took whatever vehicle was to hand as time went on—public bus, train, ferry, motor launch, airplane, taxi, and the Mercedes of our hosts in Christchurch.

AFTER YOU, MARK TWAIN

This helter-skelter approach distressed the National Travel Service, which was convinced we needed the scenic tour, to the disgust of the young man in its Auckland office who understood us and who kept shouting into the telephone as he checked schedules, "But they want to meet Kiwis!" (New Zealanders have come to be identified by the name of their famous flightless bird, which is also their nation's symbol.)

One in three New Zealanders lives in the Auckland area. A city of 820,000 located on an isthmus on the narrowest part of the North Island, Auckland has two natural harbors, opening it to the South Pacific Ocean on the east and the Tasman Sea on the west. Slow-paced, liveable, and free from air pollution, the city sprawls over more than sixty volcanic cones and craters. Rudyard Kipling wrote of it in his "Song of the Cities":

> Last, loneliest, loveliest, exquisite apart—
> On us, on us the unswerving season smiles,
> Who wonder 'mid our fern why men depart
> To seek the Happy Isles!

We boarded the city bus late one afternoon, determined to ride it to the end of the line. The end of the line was skid row. A pleasant panhandler directed Winston, who has an affinity for panhandlers, to the Bloomin' Eddy, apologizing that it was really no place for a lady. As a matter of fact it was, at least for this lady. It was the hangout for the Auckland press. As the news of our journey spread, we were surrounded by a helpful coterie of journalists offering advice on who and what to see—and what to avoid: Rotorua.

"Have you been to Yellowstone Park?"
"Yes."
"Have you been to Disneyland?"
"Yes."

JUNIOR ENGLAND: NEW ZEALAND

"Then skip Rotorua."

"Want a good place to eat? Do you like fish? Try Pelouri Jack's." (This establishment was named for a dolphin that regularly escorted ships into Auckland harbor and was protected by order of the government.)

We had already stumbled on the Railton Hotel, operated by the Salvation Army. Opened on December 13, 1961, "To the Glory of God and for the Good of the People," it was not a flophouse, but a well-run, if plain, hostelry for travellers. The Railton provided twin beds, private bath, color television, good bedside reading lights (a luxury beyond price), laundry facilities, free coffee and tea down the hall, and all the breakfast you could eat for forty dollars (New Zealand) for the two of us.

Exploring up the hill from the Railton on a sunny Sunday morning, we stopped to examine the bulletin board of the Baptist Tabernacle, the first Baptist church in Auckland, established in 1855. Its facade was in imposing, even forbidding, Greek style with six Corinthian pillars. It looked more like a post office or a bank than a church. It was eleven o'clock and Christmas carols could be heard as latecomers hastened through the double doors.

"Why not?" suggested my properly brought up spouse. We were ushered into an inconspicuous back pew. "Christ Above All," the program read. It presented a formidable schedule for the morning: three baptisms, welcome to missionaries returning from service in Papua New Guinea, music (both vocal and instrumental) by the young people, explanation of the church banners for the Sunday School, and lighting of advent candles. The Reverend D. A. K. Dickson, M.A., would deliver the sermon, "What Is a Good Man?" I shot Winston a long-suffering glance.

But it was hard to stay out of sorts with the carol singing and the enthusiasm of the parishioners, young and old. New Zealand children have faces of unparalleled rosiness and innocence. The church was packed with genuine, historic, down-to-earth, devout Kiwis. Most of the women wore hats, many of which appeared to be designed, or at least decorated, by hand. It caused us to reflect on how much has been lost to the enjoyment of Sunday churchgoers by the demise of the hat. Most of the men, even the elders, appeared tanned and muscular, and were turned out in well-tailored shorts and knee socks, and snappy, military looking safari jackets. Gorgeous bouquets of hydrangeas and agapanthus decorated the altar, the sort you would expect at a society wedding in the states. They had been grown in the gardens of the congregation and arranged by women parishioners.

It was an interesting and satisfying service, its climax a sermon of such clarity and wit that we were left in no doubt as to the attributes of a good man. As we shook hands with Mr. Dickson, he invited us to "supper" in the church basement. We accepted. The tables overflowed with delicious Kiwi cooking: casseroles, salads, and breads, and Pavlova for dessert—a meringue, covered by mounds of strawberries and all the whipped cream you could spoon over it. Many of the congregation were missionaries and former missionaries from throughout the South Seas, Asia, and even South America. Friendly, lively, and humorous conversationalists, full of spirit, well informed, and curious, the parishioners embraced us as friends and family. Without exception they approved our ambition of following Mark Twain around the equator. "Good on yer!" they agreed. We departed the church in a glow.

From Auckland we drove north toward the equator. The up-and-down hilly country, green beyond belief, was polka-dotted with sheep. New Zealand sheep look as though they've stepped out of a child's book of nursery rhymes or an advertisement for bleach. Fluffy and white, their whiteness accentuated by the intense green, they bore but faint resemblance to the idiot-faced and dingy flocks we knew at home. We stopped to buy and savor midwinter tomatoes and strawberries before cold rain and winds drove us from the highway. Rain in the tropics comes not in drops but in bulk, and the fierce wind reminded us that this midsummer December was not comparable to anything we knew in the way of weather.

Although our destination had been Whangarei (we liked the sound of it), we stopped at the Sun Valley Motor Lodge in Wellsford. It was almost as if our hosts, Sue and Bruce Alder, had been expecting us. Everything was provided for our comfort and convenience. On the dresser a card read: "Welcome to Sun Valley Motor Lodge. The articles on this tray are for your use during your stay. Please do not remove." On the tray were needles, pins, buttons, playing cards, scissors, aspirin, and bandaids.

Bruce, lean and energetic, offered to provide tea, "if you don't mind a slap-up meal." Tea proved to be a full dinner—baked chicken, potatoes mashed with chives and cottage cheese, vegetables, fruit juice, hot date and lemon pudding with ice cream—and tea. We truly didn't mind. And the "slap-up tucker," as he later enlarged on it, was delicious. We spent the rainy evening watching *Mash*, *General Hospital*, *Fantasy Island*, and *Days of Our Lives*, or parts thereof, and admiring a recurrent commercial for Decacide for lice control. We were, after all, in sheep country.

It was Bruce who introduced us to New Zealand's distinctive speech as he came and went through the downpour clad in shorts, shirt, slicker, and thongs, delivering "the morning piper," the *Waitemata Times*, and confirming the weather report, "Yis, yis, it's still rining." Sue gave the Jetsave ("Jitsave") Travel Agency "a ring" and asked Jilleen Bird to "pop in" with some brochures for us. Jilleen, a tall, amply built young woman of whole-some complexion, dressed in a pleated wool skirt, white blouse, high heels and with bare legs, was bright, inter-ested, and efficient—typical, we were to learn, of young New Zealand women.

We pressed northward to the land of the kauri tree. We live in logging country but were unprepared for the kauri. The only tree that compares with it is the California redwood. We "kodak'd" the largest remaining kauri—45.17 feet in girth and 168.99 feet tall. We saw a sawed board nineteen feet by six feet by three feet. It took twenty-two oxen to haul a single squared kauri log through the tropical swamp in which they grew. Only bullocks were used and it was said that their slow, steady pull was what did the job. Horses were useless in the muck. Early pre-chainsaw loggers felled these monster trees with Paul Bunyan-sized axes and crosscut saws twelve feet long.

Simultaneously an army of gumdiggers toiled in the mud, digging hardened blobs of kauri sap or gum from the swamps after they'd located it by probing the ground with long spears. Then they scraped and washed it, loaded it on wagons and shipped it by the thousands of tons to manufacture spar varnish, paint, and linoleum.

We saw the Bay of Islands, Doubtless Bay, and Ninety Mile Beach (actually sixty miles long), as well as the town of Kaitaia, the land for which was bought from the Maoris by missionaries in 1833 for eighty blankets, seventy axes, thirty iron pots, thirty hoes, forty plane irons, thirty pairs of scissors, thirty combs, thirty shark hooks, two thousand fish hooks, and fifty pounds of tobacco. The Maoris were both more enterprising and more practical than the Native Americans who had swapped Manhattan Island for twenty-four dollars worth of bright cloth and colored beads two hundred years earlier.

Mark Twain was charmed by the Maoris. "There is

nothing of the savage in the faces of the native chiefs ... nothing could be finer than these men's features, nothing more intellectual than these faces, nothing more masculine, nothing nobler than their aspect. ... They look like Roman patricians. ... It takes but 15 minutes to get reconciled to the tattooing, and but 15 more to perceive that it is just the thing. After that, the undecorated European face is unpleasant and ignoble."

We noticed similarities between the Maoris and the Indians in Montana. Their tradition of hospitality, for instance. John Rangihau, a contemporary Maori, writes: "We keep an open door, and anybody who moves in is always made welcome. ... We will share whatever it is that we have with them. We may not be rich, but the fact that we share with other people makes us richer ... but I am ever mindful of the fact that I am a Maori and there isn't any way through which I, as a Maori, can become a foreigner in my own land."

Maori hospitality was not extended to members of other tribes or to the *paheka*, the Maori term for missionaries and other white settlers who began coming in 1840. Tribal wars and attacks on whites made settlement and attempts at religious conversion of the locals dangerous. With these hazards compounded by the upside-down climate, strange terrain, and outlandish foliage, it was understandable that the country folks from the British Isles were disoriented. They were also hungry. New Zealand was devoid of familiar game and vegetation. Some of America's settlers were greeted by friendly Indians sharing their corn, venison, fish, and game birds. New Zealand was a land of strange marsupial animals; its only mammal was the bat. There weren't even any snakes!

Today, in spite of assured political representation in New Zealand's House of Representatives and generally enlightened race relations, the plight of the Maoris seems similar to that of Native Americans. They live on reservations or in ghettos in the cities, are poor, and have high rates of unemployment, alcoholism, and criminal convictions. Their tribal lands have frequently been traded to whites for small value.

Yet they have their own talents and humor. In a book of Maori poetry called *Something-Nothing*, I found this poem by Hone Tuwhare.

ONE-WAY TRIPPERS

Graveyards, said the learned man,
are thought to be the beginning
and the end of all our journeyings.

This may hold true of tombs which
shelter king and prince together
with their luckless concubines
and slaves. Lavish preparations
arranged by priestly travel agents,
for example, would include: diverse
weapons, bright flamingoes, chariots
with horse. Pots supplied by
thoughtful relatives were filled
with unguents and wine. Despite all
this, the learned man remarked, the
holy planners never really managed
to get the favoured person off
the ground and into space. On the
other hand, one can say with certainty
that lowly folks who occupy less opulent
and unpretentious graves couldn't get
a lousy third-class travel permit.
But one conclusive fact impresses me:
They all are dead.

JUNIOR ENGLAND: NEW ZEALAND

Tourists find the Maoris interesting and flock to Rotorua to see them perform and demonstrate their carving and weaving. Recently, enterprising Maoris, hoping to lure American dollars, have proposed to build and manage tourist accommodations resembling Maori palaces rather than Sheraton Hotels. The New Zealand government is backing the enterprise. It sounds like a good idea. I can think of few experiences more exotic than bunking in a Maori palace and sauntering out to view the launching of that most impressive of all Maori artifacts, a canoe with stands for eighty rowers and numerous warriors. This warship, housed on rail tracks at Waitanga, is launched only once a year. We didn't find out when or on what occasion. But when the palace is finished and the canoe is to be launched, we intend to be there.

* * *

At Hamilton, a city of 100,000 south of Auckland, the English gardens began in earnest. Traffic dividers were nosegays of begonias, marigolds, sweet william, ageratum, and roses. The farms became more prosperous. "It was Junior England all the way to Christ Church—in fact, just a garden," wrote Mark Twain.

A handsome couple on the bus told us they had emigrated to New Zealand from England in 1950. Postwar opportunities in England were bleak and future possibilities for their children even bleaker; the climate of the British Isles was dismal; they were adventurers. They expressed the impression that New Zealanders' devotion to the mother country had lessened since their islands had achieved dominion status in 1947.

Perhaps so, but we noticed that the New Zealand press and television reported almost daily on the pregnancies and costumes of Princess Di, who seemed to be held in reverence by all except the authors of *The Kiwi Joker Book*. We met a woman who had served as president of the Victoria League, an organization which she said was formed "to keep us in touch with the Motherland." I asked whether, as Mark Twain noticed, New Zealanders still referred to England as home. "Of course not," she replied, only to explain in the next sentence that one of the projects of the Victoria League was "sending lamb home to England."

The country from Hamilton to Lake Taupo was pleasant, through good farm land, vegetable gardens, and vast areas of introduced forest. The Monterey pine, imported from California, has become New Zealand's most important tree. It grows twice as fast here as on the U.S. west coast, because of the ample rainfall and warm climate. Planted in rows, some on such steep hillsides that workers have to be suspended by ropes, the forests march over the landscape like armies.

Golf courses along the way were mowed and fertilized by grazing sheep, which, we surmised, would not be nearly as vulnerable to golf balls as greenskeepers. The sheep were kept off the greens by electric fences. We didn't find out how many strokes a golfer is penalized for striking a sheep, or if they are considered natural hazards.

All the land in New Zealand seems to have been put to optimum use. There are deer farms and rabbit ranches to make use of forage which would otherwise be wasted. Even geysers and thermal springs have been harnessed to produce geothermal energy. Clever, enterprising, and hardworking, these New Zealanders.

Before all this could be accomplished, it was necessary to destroy the face of New Zealand. Ship passengers halfway across the Tasman Sea in the last century could smell New Zealand burning. The beautiful native forests and bush were tamed by the axe and the match. In great "drives," one tree was aimed to hit another partly cut tree, which smashed into another downhill, and soon to a gully bottom. Left to dry during the summer, they were lit after Christmas. Sparks flew for miles. After the bushburn, the settlers changed the face of New Zealand by sowing the country with a mixture of perennial grasses, clover, and turnipseed. Years later, today's green pastures and white sheep appeared.

Lake Taupo is almost at the center of the North Island. Ian Osborne, proprietor of the SunSeeker Motel, picked us up at the bus stop. Handsome, lean, cordial, he drove us through the Lake Taupo botanical garden (no town in New Zealand is too small to have a botanical garden); past the spectacular Huka Falls on the Waikato River, to the Wairakei thermal valley, the largest geothermal power project in the world; and along the shore of New Zealand's largest lake. The lakeshore of Lake Taupo is Maori property.

Ian pointed out Maori land which had been cleared, cultivated, and planted to forest under government auspices, but is fast returning to bush. Hardworking New Zealanders like Ian and his wife, Nola, have little patience with the Maoris (whom Ian called "Marys"). The problem, according to Ian, is that the "Marys" don't like to work but prefer to live in the bush of their ancestral land as they did before the time of the paheka.

At twilight, we watched from our motel windows as a hailstorm swept up the lake, followed by clearing and a rainbow which framed the steam rising from a volcanic peak at the far end of Lake Taupo. That night the state ceremony for the burial of Sir Keith Kolysake, a former prime minister whose ancestry included Maori blood, was aired on television. The New Zealand flag and a Maori feathered cloak enshrouded the casket. Members of the TeAtianea tribe delivered the *karanga* mourning cry on the steps of the parliament building and at the cathedral—an eerie and moving tribute.

We had time the next morning, while waiting for our bus, to wander through the Taupo Rose Garden, "established with 800 bushes budded, reared and planted by the ladies of the Taupo Rose Society." The fountain, bird bath, sundial and stonework were donated by "the patroness and other generous members. Enjoy it in peace." We did. No one was about. Not a blade of grass was out of place in the garden nor on the adjoining bowling green where white-clad oldsters performed a skilled but restrained ceremony which we had never before witnessed. Nearby were the Senior Citizens Association, the Regional Museum and Art Gallery, public library, town hall, and police station.

Wellington, the capital, is a city on a hillside overlooking a beautiful harbor. That seems to be the description of every major New Zealand city. Combine this with the British devotion to cozy homes and flower gardens, and a miracle is created. In the morning sunshine after an evening downpour, Wellington was not only newly washed, sparkling, and beautiful; it was simply dazzling.

The DeBeers Hotel is elderly, cheap, and well located in the downtown area. After breakfast we walked to the capitol—actually there are three: the modest old colonial edifice, a second building which looks like a capitol, and a five-year-old structure resembling a layered cake. The Kiwis call this "the beehive" and claim it is better adapted to honey making than governance. Here the governor-general reads, in the absence of the Queen, the Speech from the Throne, and gives the royal assent to legislation, a gambit that mystifies Americans.

New Zealand is a sovereign independent state, with a parliamentary government and a constitutional monarchy. The Crown of New Zealand is separate from that of Great

JUNIOR ENGLAND: NEW ZEALAND

Britain, but is vested in the same person, Queen Elizabeth II. Health services, most of them supported by the state, are available to all New Zealanders. Most medicines and prenatal and maternity services are free. Free dental care is provided for children and adolescents. A comprehensive system of social security ensures that all citizens have a reasonable standard of living.

New Zealand's parliament extended to women the right to vote in 1893. The nineteenth amendment to the United States Constitution, giving nationwide suffrage to women, did not go into effect until August 20, 1920. Mark Twain, an ardent supporter of women's suffrage, observed:

> Here is a remark I take from the official report: "A feature of the election was the orderliness and sobriety of the people. Women were in no way molested."
>
> At home, a standing argument against woman suffrage has always been that women could not go to the polls without being insulted. The arguments against woman suffrage have always taken the easy form of prophecy. ... Men ought to begin to feel a sort of respect for their mothers and wives and sisters by this time. ... In the New Zealand law occurs this: "The word *person* whenever it occurs throughout the Act includes *woman.*"
>
> That is a promotion, you see. By that enlargement of the word, the matron with the garnered wisdom and experience of fifty years becomes at one jump the political equal of her callow kid of 21.

Window-shopping the posh stores of Wellington's business district, we were impressed by the display of fashionable merchandise. It made us wonder where New Zealand women buy their hats. Not in these stores. We were startled by a sign in a meat market window: "Closed from December 23 to January 9." It was now December 14. Kiwis take their holiday observance seriously.

AFTER YOU, MARK TWAIN

The society page of the *Wellington Dominion* provided good reading. We clipped the following nuptial account by Prue Dashfield under the headline Tizard Wedding in Gardens:

Counting newly-weds Bob Tizard and Mary Nacey, minister, witnesses, guests and two one-year-old boys, the wedding party totalled nine.

But the short, affectionate service celebrated yesterday by Wanganui Member of Parliament Russell Marshall wasn't quite as private as they planned. Which was very private. As soon as you invited someone, someone else was offended, Mr. Tizard said. "I wanted something private for Bob," Ms. Nacey said. "Just to have a small thing." Her mother wasn't there.

But a television crew, three reporters and two photographers were, clustered on the bride's side of the fountain in Wellington's lush Botanic Gardens.

Ms. Nacey wore turquoise and pink silk. Labour MP Mr. Tizard wore a brown suit, a red carnation and their son, Joseph, 20 months, on his hip while he exchanged vows and wedding rings with his wife.

Joseph was attired for the occasion of his parents' wedding in blue and yellow overalls and carried a yellow and red carnation in his capacity as flower boy. "There's no sexism here," said his mother. The other flower boy was David Robinson, 15 months, the son of Ms. Nacey's friend, Liz Wilson, a witness to the marriage along with Mr. Tizard's parliamentary colleague, Sir Basil Arthur.

Ms. Nacey said the marriage was an affirmation. "We've put up with each other for four years." It was a second marriage for the former deputy prime minister and minister of finance, Mr. Tizard. Cath Tizard, his first wife, is now mayor of Auckland.

Ms. Nacey, who was as approachable and candid a bride as her side of the fountain could have asked for, said she hadn't made her mind up on the post-marital surname. "I was thinking of Nacey-Tizard but friends of mine thought it sounded like a pesticide." But she might adopt that or she might stick with the name she's had for 30 years.

"I still want to be regarded as myself, not just an appendage," she said. "I certainly won't be Mary Tizard."

"There are too many Tizard women at the moment," said her husband.

JUNIOR ENGLAND: NEW ZEALAND

> ... The wedding party was celebrating last night with
> a slap-up meal at an Italian restaurant, the only one they
> could take the children to, Ms. Nacey said.

There was a three-column photo of the smiling couple and their blonde son.

We were reluctant to board the ferry for the crossing to Picton and the South Island. The view of the capital from the water was spectacular—San Francisco in miniature, and clearer air. Luckily we fell in with two more of those wonderful grande dames in serviceable hats, drinking beer in the bar. Bound for Dunedin at the tip of the South Island, where their Scottish ancestors had come 150 years ago to raise sheep, they confessed that it was such as they who are the backbone of New Zealand.

SERVICEABLE HATS

37

AFTER YOU, MARK TWAIN

Europeans who had immigrated since World War II, they said, were "not workers like the old settlers."

"Do you tip?" they asked. "Don't. It will spoil everything." Although we had been guilty of tipping, we recalled that the tourism booklet "About New Zealand" had said, "Tips are not expected, nor is any service charge added to hotel accounts."

Our assigned seating compartment was shared with a sad young couple and their year-old baby, swaddled in fleece in a "push chair" (stroller), as are all New Zealand babies. The father, a policeman, was being transferred from Auckland to Hull—about the length of New Zealand. They were fearful and reluctant to make such a change away from family and friends and at such a vast distance. New Zealand police are organized and posted by federal authorities.

The train from the ferry landing at Picton to Christchurch was rattly, uncomfortable, and slow, a poor choice, but we wanted to try one New Zealand train.

* * *

It was December 18. On the radio a Maori choir was singing "Joy to the World" with a jive rhythm and strong drum accompaniment. We caught an early bus from Christchurch south and west to Queenstown, the Southern Alps, and the fjords of Milford Sound. December, January, and February are summer here, but it was raining and a cold wind was blowing off the Antarctic. We wore our warmest clothes and raingear.

We hadn't expected the stop at the Mackenzie Basin Hydroelectric Project to be so interesting. A series of dams, conduits, and canals linking the Waitaki River and Lakes Tekapo, Pukaki, and Ohau, this enormous project was begun in 1928 and is still in the process of expansion. Glacial runoff from the Southern Alps makes the water milky green. Since New Zealand has no nuclear power plants, and imported petroleum furnishes almost half of the country's needs, hydroelectric power is invaluable. Parks, recreation areas, scenic roads, "caravan" (motor home) and tenting facilities, as well as swimming and boating areas, and unobtrusive landscaping are included in the complex, making it a major tourist center. One of our fellow passengers, a young civil engineer from British Columbia, was so intrigued with the layout that he almost missed the bus.

We followed glacial streams over the continental divide, through fields of beautiful lavendar, blue, and pink lupine-like flowers. According to our courier, a woman settler wishing to beautify the area had broadcast the seeds, and over the years the plants had colonized the valleys. This is the season when they "flare," he said. Later a park naturalist identified them as policeman's helmet and called them invaders. They've become a noxious weed crowding out natural forage and, in the dry season, become a fire hazard. The woman's effort to imitate the English countryside backfired.

Queenstown was socked in. Since our flight to see the fjords of Milford Sound was cancelled, we took the gondola to the top of the mountain overlooking the city to catch a glimpse of a stark, treeless range of mountains called the Remarkables to the east. Descending, we strolled through a cemetery where the early-day Irish were separated by a narrow roadway from the Scots, apparently in the hope that the Creator would recognize the difference between Catholics and Protestants on Judgment Day. An afternoon steamship cruise on Lake Wakatipu and an obligatory tourist excursion to a sheep station filled the day.

The combined church choirs and Sunday schools of Queenstown announced their annual Christmas pageant at St. Paul's Anglican Church. We joined the assembled congregation, which overflowed the tiny stone building, for carol singing and reading of the Christmas story. It was a dandy pageant. A baby was jiggled enthusiastically by a conscientious little Mary in a blue veil. A New Zealand lamb immortalized by a taxidermist attended the cradle. The youthful shepherds were equipped with genuine shepherds' crooks. The wise men had the proper bathrobes, and all the little boys came scuffling and jumping out of the church at the recessional. Briefly homesick, we could have been at any of dozens of Christmas pageants we've attended over the years. It was cold. The Kiwis, wearing only light sweaters, seemed not to notice and heartily wished us a merry Christmas as we left the church shivering in our layered woolens and raincoats.

In the morning we headed north. Public bus is surely the best way to see the South Island's western shore. Along this coastline the warm water of the Tasman Sea rises and turns to rain, then to snow when it hits the high mountains. In short order jungle vegetation gives way to snow-capped mountains. Everywhere were signs of flooding from a recent storm and accompanying snow melt. (In March 1982, *six feet* of rain fell here in three days, we were told.) When the sun comes out, the country steams.

We had been looking forward to the drive up the coast, but the sea was almost never in sight until suddenly the road left the forest to follow the shoreline. The sky was blue and declared a bonus of unexpected rainbows. To our right were snowy mountain peaks and glacial lakes. To our left the great waves of the Tasman Sea were coming in, mile after mile, like lace fans.

"Trampers" with heavy backpacks, shorts, and skivvies, got on and off the bus at unpredictable stops between the Tasman Sea and the Southern Alps. In New

JUNIOR ENGLAND: NEW ZEALAND

Zealand trails are called tracks and hikers are called trampers. They looked pale and pooped. I overheard one say, "At first I was afraid I was going to die, and after a while I was afraid I wouldn't." They were a dramatic contrast to the tanned and robust hikers we encounter on the high, arid trails of Glacier National Park. We were reminded that the New Zealander, Sir Edmund Hilary, the first to conquer Mt. Everest, learned mountaineering in the Southern Alps.

The next day we, too, became trampers—on the Terrace-Tatare Track over an old gold sluicing operation. It's hard to imagine how people ever discovered gold in this undergrowth, much less how they extracted it. As with all mining operations, a mess remained—piles of tailings left by dredges, hillsides gnawed by hydraulic sluicing. Through the dim light, the devastation could barely be made out under the foliage. We barely saw the sky or sunlight. There were no flowers or birds—just moss-covered trees, none very high, and vines, ferns, and dense undergrowth. There were no vistas—just one overview of a vast floodplain.

Mark Twain agreed: "There is nothing like surface mining to snatch the graces and beauties and benignities out of a paradise, and make an odious and repulsive spectacle of it."

Tucked away down the road from the visitor center, we came upon tiny St. James Anglican Church, its altar backdrop a picture window framing Fox Glacier. This was pictured on New Zealand's "Peace" issue of postage stamps, commemorating the end of World War II and expressing "the spirit of thankfulness and the true Christian hope to banish permanently the horrors of war." A postage stamp seemed a uniquely New Zealand kind of war memorial. The unattended church with its blue carpeting and draperies is lovely. To one side of the

41

altar, a weaving by a local woman is a replica of the stamp.

In the late afternoon we took a white-knuckle ski plane ride over Fox and Franz Josef glaciers, flying frighteningly close to deep blue crevasses. To my way of thinking, glaciers are much better admired shining in their cirques from the bottom of a mountain. Returning across the island to Christchurch, we skirted Arthur's Pass National Park and followed the Otira Gorge road, memorialized in verse by the Reverend Tremayne Curnow, vicar of Malvern in the mid-1920s. His poem was published in the *Christchurch Press* while we were there. The vicar frequently rode in a horse-drawn coach over the steep mountain road before construction of a railroad tunnel.

THE BALLAD OF OTIRA GORGE

Upon the topmost seat I ride
Ladies and baggage go inside
And as we cross the great divide
My collar forms a funnel
To catch the rain which wets me through
Don't gush to me about the view
I'm cold and wet so tell me do
When shall we have the tunnel?

The view it fairly scares me stiff
The road's a ledge along a cliff
The wheels go near it, heavens if
They make a deviation
I only hope that I survive
This perfect nightmare of a drive
To offer thanks when I arrive
Safe at Otira station.

JUNIOR ENGLAND: NEW ZEALAND

The driver tries to calm my fears
As round a hairpin bend he steers
There's been no accident for years
He hastens to assure me.
I've done this job in wind and rain
Three times a week and back again
For eighteen years, but all in vain
This has no comfort for me.

I'm no seeker after thrills
I'd rather travel under hills
Than over them with rain and chills
In constant trepidation.
I only hope some other day
To travel back the tunnel way
So may no further hitch delay
That blessed perforation.

New Zealand names, British and Maori, are a puzzle
to the newcomer. I made out a pattern to the nomencla-
ture by studying the map. Major cities and towns have
British names: Auckland, Hamilton, Stratford, Christchurch,
New Plymouth, Palmerston North, Bluff, Cambridge.
Smaller cities and towns have Maori names: Papakura,
Wanganui, Whangarei, Te Puke, Opotiki, Papatoetoe,
Waiuku, Kaitangata, Whangamata.

Mountains have British names: Cook, Brewster,
Kepler, Stuart, Cameron, Aspiring, Egmont, the
Remarkables, Spencer, Hopkins, Murchison, Owen, and
even Gentle Annie Hill. Lakes have Maori names: Taupo,
Waikaremoana, Wanaka, Hawea, Waitaki, Rotorua,
Pukaki, Ohau, Hauroko, Manapouri, TeAnau.

Bays and capes and other appurtenances of the
seacoast have British names: Bay of Plenty, Great Exhi-
bition Bay, Cape Farewell, Separation Point, Jackson

AFTER YOU, MARK TWAIN

Bay, Hawke Bay, Cape Turnagain, Bay of Islands. Rivers have Maori names: Rakaia, Rangitata, Karamea, Wanganui, Rangitaiki, Whangaehu.

Memorials! Memorials! On North Island and South Island, in every town square, in every church, in every park, in every museum there are monuments, markers, tablets, columns, monoliths, obelisks, cairns, cenotaphs, arches, and bridges in memory of the war dead; as we found at St. James, there's even a postage stamp. From the Maori wars to the Falkland Islands, the Kiwis have laid down their lives for the glory of the British Empire. New Zealand sent 6,495 officers and men to the Boer War in South Africa in 1899–1902. The famous Australian and New Zealand Army Corps (Anzac) lost 16,697 men in France in World War I. In World War II, more than ten thousand were killed, almost twenty thousand wounded, and eight thousand taken prisoner. New Zealanders fought as well in Korea and Vietnam. New Zealand has lost proportionately more men in war than any other western nation.

The usual inscription: "Justice–Peace–Sacrifice. To the glory of God—in memory of the men and women of New Zealand who laid down their lives in war." On a memorial dedicated to those who fell in the Great War and ending with the plea, "Give peace in our time, O Lord," we noticed that by the time it was dedicated, World War II had already begun. The Bridge of Remembrance over the Avon River in Christchurch honors "the soldiers of Canterbury [County] who have marched over it to three wars." On a pillar near an ocean beach near Christchurch was a new bronze plaque to those who fell in the Falklands, with the inscription: "Lest We Forget."

The memorials date back a good while in some instances. Mark Twain noted a couple of curious ones at Wanganui.

JUNIOR ENGLAND: NEW ZEALAND

One is in honor of white men "who fell in defense of law and order against fanaticism and barbarism." Fanatacism. ... It is right to praise these brave white men who fell in the Maori war—they deserve it; but the presence of that word detracts from the dignity of their cause and their deeds, and makes them appear to have spilled their blood in a conflict with ignoble men, men not worthy of that costly sacrifice. But the men *were* worthy. It was no shame to fight them. They fought for their homes, they fought for their country; they bravely fought and bravely fell; and it would take nothing from the honor of the brave Englishmen who lie under the monument, but *add* to it, to say that they died in defense of English laws and English homes against men worthy of the sacrifice—the Maori patriots.

It isn't only foreigners who have noticed this profusion of war monuments. Jim Henderson writes in *The New Zealanders:*

> They've sown war memorials all over New Zealand, from one end to the other, the steel tentacles of war reaching even into the almost tangible peace of Halfmoon Bay, Stewart Island, so unfairly, it seems. ... I've just finished reading and re-reading an incredible sentence from a souvenir booklet, "Our Little Bit," published by the New Zealand YMCA in the Field in France, 1918, the war still on: "If we all die, if all the men of our race and our generation die, it is a small thing, and not worthy of consideration, if we can help purchase for other nations that freedom which we of New Zealand so passionately love, so freely enjoy."
> When do we begin to *live* for our little country, for our little unacknowledged World?

Small wonder that New Zealanders have cried, "Enough!" By a majority of 70 percent they voted to create a nuclear-free zone in the South Pacific and to refuse access to nuclear-powered and nuclear-armed warships. While we were there, a U.S. battleship was prevented from docking in Auckland harbor. The young couple who hosted our Christmas stay in Christchurch had pursued "peace studies" in England and are currently active in the antinuclear movement. Both are fifth-generation New Zealanders, descendants of the country's missionary and military traditions. They are devoted to peaceful resolutions and working to preserve a nuclear-free future for their three children, their country, their part of the South Pacific, and the planet.

Item in the *Auckland Star* of November 19, 1895: "On Friday evening last Mark Twain was entertained by the Savage Club in Christchurch at a grand banquet in the Municipal Chambers. A large company consisting of the leading members of the Press, the Bar, Art, Science and Society gave him a really royal reception. Besides being the greatest success on the lecture platform, Mark Twain is an unprecedented social success."

Christchurch is our favorite New Zealand city. It is beautiful, and so reminiscent of England that it seemed to call for a certain British reserve. But the Sunday book review section of the *Christchurch Press* reviewed three publications under the headline: "All Bound Up With Sex." They were *The Bounder's Companion*; *The Art of Coarse Sex*, dedicated to Lady Chatterley's husband; and *How to Regain Your Virginity*, outlining a maintenance program for virginity (complete with the Virginity Hotline Number staffed twenty-four hours a day by virgins).

John Boanes, our Christmas host, introduced us to *The Kiwi Joker Book: A Guide to the Real New Zealand Joker*, by Gavin Wainright. The chainsaw is the talisman of today's macho descendant of the pioneer logger, who fully expects to marry a "sheila" who is an experienced virgin. "After the bar closed at six, he'd go home, sink a few more beers, and watch the tele. Then he'd hit the sack. Sunday he had a friendly grudge match jacked up, and a few more flagons promised after he helped a mate chainsaw a nearby stand of kauris that blocked the view of the local tip ... a joker knew what life was all about." The New Zealand Joker and his sheila were hilariously depicted in a raunchy musical called "Footrot Flats," lampooning life on a dried-out New Zealand sheep station.

We spent an afternoon wandering through the 450-acre botanical garden, Hagley Park, and took "set tea" with the city's grande dames (in hats) and, surprisingly, businessmen, at the Gardens Restaurant. The Canterbury Museum adjoins the garden and houses an Antarctic exploration wing with memorabilia of early expeditions, as well as the up-to-date equipment. Most Antarctic expeditions leave from Christchurch.

A statue of Robert Falcon Scott, leader of British expeditions to the Antarctic, is centrally located on the bank of the Avon River which meanders through the town. Scott and his party reached the South Pole on January 25, 1912. That all had perished on the return journey was not learned until a year later. The statue of Scott in polar dress, grasping an alpenstock and facing north as on his homeward journey, carries the last entry from his diary: "We are weak—writing is difficult—but, for my own sake, I do not regret this journey, which shows that Englishmen can endure hardships, help one another, and meet death with as great fortitude as ever in the past."

In December 1955, a U.S. Navy expedition to the South Pole dedicated a nearby memorial: "To strive, to seek, to find, and not to yield. Dedicated to the memory of the brave Antarctic explorers whose valor and determination showed the way for all those who now venture in their wake."

We left Christchurch for Australia on Boxing Day, the day after Christmas, a holiday everywhere in the British Commonwealth.

CHAPTER IV

A Sweltering Day
in Australia

Australia is a large country with a small population. No one goes there by chance, for it is not on the way to anywhere else.

Ian Bevan,
The Sunburnt Country (London, 1954)

It was raining. We were tired. We spent the day in our room at the Menzies Hotel in Sydney drinking tea and reading the local newspapers, getting up strength to tackle the continent-sized country of Australia. You can learn a lot about a country from its newspapers.

- The *Australian* was serializing William Manchester's J. F. Kennedy biography, *One Bright, Shining Moment.*
- There were four pages of horse racing results in the *Sydney Morning Herald.*
- Some 250 male "hunks," ages eighteen to forty-six, showed up at a Sydney hotel room in answer to an advertisement for good-looking men willing to pose nude for *Playgirl* magazine.
- Australians were on a high. Their tennis players

had won the Davis Cup; their yacht, Australia II, had brought home the America's Cup; and championships ranging from rugby to the world marathon title were being celebrated. Sports here are a national institution. Not to be interested in sports is synonymous with degeneracy. Next to sports, gambling is a major preoccupation—lotteries, slot machines, horse racing, bingo. Australians spend more on gambling than on defense. And enjoy it more.

- A woman from the island of Tasmania castigated the president of the Australian Wool Council in a letter to the editor for refusing to appoint a woman to the Wool Board, and for saying, "Not a lot of women in Australia know anything about the Australian wool industry." The letter, headed "Wool Over Eyes About Women," pointed out that women are not only the spinners, knitters, and handknit designers, but also that many are active sheep farmers and woolgrowers.

- A breakthrough in lychee packaging promised an export crop to rival New Zealand's kiwi fruit. By dipping the delicate lychees into heated fungicide and sealing them in plastic, shippers could deliver them flawless and fresh in China. If this seems like carrying coals to Newcastle, there's a shortage of lychees in China during the New Year celebration.

- The National Aboriginal Conference, citing prior ownership and sovereignty, claimed that Western Australia should be ceded to present-day Aborigines.

- The French magazine, *L'Exprès*, had named Australia country of the year: "No other country, no other eldorado in the world, can express or incarnate to such a point the hopes, the aspirations of the old world. ... Australia is perhaps the last dream of the decade, the end of the voyage, certainly the last frontier ... the last refuge where, far from the torments of old Europe and the noise of war between a tired West and an East which has nothing to offer, life is still good."

- The British aircraft carrier HMS *Invincible* lay in Sydney harbor in need of repairs but forbidden to dock or be serviced because of suspected nuclear armaments. In Australia, as in New Zealand, there is strong opposition to both nuclear power and nuclear weapons.
- Although a million applications to immigrate had been received the previous year, Australia remained selectively underpopulated. It welcomed white, unskilled workers from Britain, Greece, and Italy to work in mines, factories, and service industries after World War II, but it now seeks only skilled and professional workers. Prime Minister Robert Hawke said: "We don't want people here just so they can join the end of a dole queue."
- Only about 9 percent of Australians are Asian. The country is determined not to become an Asian country. Japan is Australia's number one market for agricultural, energy, and mineral exports. More Australians per capita are learning Japanese than any other nationality.

We had obviously been wise to rest a day before "having a go" at the Australians. Like most Americans, we were ignorant about Australia. In grade school we learned the names of the continents. But on the map of our long-ago geography book we recalled Australia only as a rather strangely shaped island somewhere down there on the bottom. It doesn't seem possible that it has grown to be about the same size as mainland United

A SWELTERING DAY IN AUSTRALIA

States. The country is a quarry and a farm. Self-sufficient in minerals—bauxite, copper, diamonds, gold, iron, lead, nickel, uranium, zinc, and coal—it soon will also supply all its own oil and gas. For the moment, like New Zealand, it is said to ride on the sheep's back in wool and mutton exports. It has been successfully exporting films, novels, and pop singers, as well as athletes.

Living in Australia is like living in a gym. The fit, sunbronzed population, a natural byproduct of a sunny climate and a 12,210-mile coastline (including two beaches ninety miles long), appears to be made up of surfers and sailors, cricketers, and tennis players, who have no need to resort to diet clubs or exercise machines. In their spare time they garden. Sydney's suburb of Manly, a thirty-five-minute ferry ride across the bay, got its name from the fine physiques of the Aborigines who were canoeing in the surf when the first Britishers arrived. Today Manly and its beaches are filled with surfers, artists, performers, and those the Aussies call "dotty people."

Gloria Boes, a friendly traveller we'd met in New Zealand, invited us to her club in Manly. It was not the sort of club we expected. Set on a promontory overlooking the harbor, the Manly Club for Returned Servicemen boasts more "poker" (slot) machines than we'd seen outside Las Vegas. Flooded with sunlight, the club at midday was well patronized by both men and women, glasses of beer beside them, enthusiastically cranking one-armed bandits. The sinister dinginess and bad air of Las Vegas were missing, and seemed not to be necessary for the enjoyment of gambling.

The club, with membership in the thousands at ten dollars a year, makes enough from its "pokies" for a swimming pool, tennis courts, billiard room, squash courts, steam rooms, gymnasiums, bowling alleys, restaurant, and bar. There are regular dances. Everybody goes. People dress however they please. Everybody has a good time.

Almost all of Australia's population of fifteen million is crowded into a narrow strip along the east coast and a tiny section of the southwest corner of the continent. The two major cities, Sydney and Melbourne, each have populations between two and a half and three million. Less than 20 percent of the people live in rural areas.

Mark Twain found that Australians resembled Americans. "The people have easy and cordial manners from the beginning. ... This is American. To put it another way, it is English friendliness with the English shyness and self-consciousness left out. ... Australia is strictly democratic and reserves and restraints are things that are bred by differences of rank."

Politically it is certainly one of the freest and most democratic of countries. Voting is compulsory. Those who fail to vote are fined! It is almost democratic to a fault. "To appear ordinary, just like everybody else, is sometimes a necessity for success," says newspaperman Donald Horne, author of The *Lucky Country*. "What often perishes altogether—in the bureaucracies of business or of government or in the universities and in such intellectual communities as exist—are originality, insight, and sensitivity, the creative sources of human activity."

A laid-back lifestyle is indigenous. Lying in bikinis, topless, or in the altogether on the sand under a carcinogenic sun is the universal sport. Australians drink 22.5 gallons of strong (and good—try Fosters) beer per head per year. In this non-competitive society, their attitude toward work is summed up by the popular bumper sticker, "I'd rather be surfing." There is widespread indifference to religion. Australians relish the good life as exemplified by the Polynesians.

But the first settlers had little appreciation for the lifestyle or culture of the Aborigines, whom they looked

A SWELTERING DAY IN AUSTRALIA

THE OLD SETTLERS

upon as little more than animals, and whom they sometimes hunted for sport. Mark Twain noted that the Aborigines, who may have numbered about 150,000 in 1788, had practiced infanticide, but that "the white man knew ways of reducing a native population 80 percent in 20 years. The native had never seen anything as fine as that before."

Twain philosophized, "The Whites always mean well when they take human fish out of the ocean and try to make them dry and warm and happy and comfortable in a chicken coop; but the kindest-hearted white man can always be depended on to prove himself inadequate when he deals with savages. ... If he had any wisdom he would know that his own civilization is a hell to the savage—but he hasn't any, and has never had any; and for lack of it he shut up those poor natives in the unimaginable perdition of his civilization, committing his crime with the very best intentions, and saw those poor creatures waste away under his tortures; and gazed at it, vaguely troubled and sorrowful, and wondered what could be the matter with them."

"There are many humorous things in the world," Mark Twain observed, "among them the white man's notion that he is less savage than other savages."

Today's remaining Aborigines must have been equally impressed by the recent finding of an Australian royal commission that the British government decades ago secretly conducted atomic weapons tests in their homelands, leaving dangerous plutonium and other radioactive contamination. The Australian government is attempting to force Britain to compensate the Aborigines and pay for clean-up of the site.

"I'm going to write a book on Australia," Mark Twain called out to a reporter over the railing of his ship as it docked in Sydney harbor on September 16, 1895. "I

A SWELTERING DAY IN AUSTRALIA

think I ought to start now. You know so much more of a country when you haven't seen it than when you have. Besides, you don't get your mind strengthened by contact with the hard facts of things. The hardest facts for people who visit foreign places are the local liars. They come out and stuff you with information you don't want and this fouls your memory ever after. ... What are my ideas and impressions in coming to Australia? I don't know. I'm ready to adopt any that seem handy. I don't believe in going outside accepted views. If there are any little things, for instance, that you would like to work off on me, fire away."

Sydney Harbor impressed Mark Twain: "We went oh-ing and ah-ing in admiration up through the crooks and turns of the spacious and beautiful harbor—a harbor which is the darling of Sydney and the wonder of the world." A showplace today, it was originally the setting for adversity. When the American revolution made it necessary for Great Britain to find a new place to ship undesirables, it turned to Australia to relieve the overcrowding of the "gaols." Australia was ideally suited: it was so far from any other "civilized" place that escape would be difficult; the climate was mild; and there was little chance of opposition from the natives. Most of England's criminals and misfits, earlier destined to become Americans, were confined at a penal colony known as The Rocks. In 1788 eleven prison ships arrived at Sydney Harbor carrying 717 convicts, of whom 180 were women. Being descended from these early arrivals is the Australian equivalent of having had ancestors who came to North America on the *Mayflower*. In fifty-three years the colony of New South Wales received eighty-three thousand prisoners.

Gradually, the original squalor of The Rocks gave way to brothels and saloons and warehouses. Today it has become a tourist attraction rivalling Quincy Market in Boston. Where once convicts were chained and beaten with a cat-o'-nine-tails, now boutiques, design studios, restaurants, and crafts stores offer everything from boomerangs to art deco.

The Sydney Opera House is mounted like a jewel in this harbor setting. Designed by Danish architect Jorn Utzon, it was officially opened by Queen Elizabeth II in 1973, after much controversy and costs that soared from initial projections of seven million dollars (Australian) to more than one hundred million. (In true club-Aussie fashion, the shortfall was made up by a series of opera house lotteries.)

Everybody got in on the act. Australia's Dame Joan Sutherland, internationally acclaimed operatic soprano, questioned the acoustics. Shortage of parking raised another outcry, and the mounting costs outraged the frugal (which included almost everybody). A cartoonist drew turtle heads coming out of the nested shells of the structure. In the midst of the recriminations and long before the opening, the architect quit and left town. Later he sued, and collected, for unpaid design fees.

A committee of local architects was appointed to complete the building's interiors. But when they scrapped Utzon's designs, a movement was mounted to bring Utzon back. It is said that by comparison with the Sydney Opera House, erecting the Empire State Building was as simple as building a garage. But whatever the cost or anguish, Sydney and Australia acquired an art object of incomparable worth—a huge outdoor sculpture.

We got the last two seats for the opening night of the summer opera season on January 7. Seated in the back row of a box, we saw the *dinky-di*, the elite, of New South Wales decked out in formal attire for Verdi's *Rigoletto*. We also saw what was wrong with the opera house. We caught only an occasional glimpse of what must have been a brilliant performance.

Later we returned to the opera house for Japanese/Sydney Friendship festivities; for a wonderful free two-piano concert in a secluded theater; for a chance conversation over drinks on the sun-filled plaza with a delightful couple from Melbourne; and to witness the start of the annual Sydney–Hobart yacht race, a glorious pageant of excitement and color as the flotilla set sail. The harbor is a focal point for public events.

Sydney Harbor's most poignant story is of the disaster of the *Duncan Dunbar*, called by Mark Twain, "one of the most pathetic tragedies in the history of that pitiless ruffian, the sea." The great natural harbor is hidden by Sydney Heads, two bluffs near a false break in the shoreline sometimes mistaken for the harbor entrance, particularly at night in the time before it was lighted. The fine sailing ship *Duncan Dunbar* was bringing back long-awaited daughters who had been sent "home to England" for schooling, as was the tradition in colonial days. Returning with them were their mothers.

Twain made the most of the story: "The wind lost force, or there was a miscalculation, and before the Heads were sighted the darkness came on. It was said that ordinarily the captain would have waited for the morning; but this was no ordinary occasion; all about him were appealing faces, faces pathetic with disappointment. So his sympathy moved him to try the dangerous passage in the dark. He had entered the Heads seventeen times, and believed he knew the ground. So he steered straight for the false opening, mistaking it for the true one. He did not find out that he was wrong until it was too late. ... Not one of all that fair and gracious company was ever seen again alive. The tale is told to every stranger that passes the spot, and it will continue to be told to all that come, for generations. ..."

AFTER YOU, MARK TWAIN

Sure enough, our friend Gloria Boes, told us the story of the shipwreck of the *Duncan Dunbar*, which sank on August 20, 1857, with 121 people on board. She pointed out the spot where the wreckage of the ship had been visible when she was a girl.

The *Sydney Morning Herald* reported after Twain's first lecture: "'My experience amongst lawyers and bars, newspaper editors, horsethieves and congressmen,' these were the reminiscences that Mark Twain related at the beginning of his Saturday lecture. The hall was packed to suffocation and it screamed at his thoroughly Twainesque linking together of opposites. ... But just what makes the success of these comic extracts from a human diary that is crowded with incident makes it also impossible to reproduce any idea of the effect of them. The manner of relation is so good, so skillfully adapted to drive the points home, the side touches are so deftly placed, and the discursive philosophy of the lecturer so omnipresent, that description is easily outdone. Besides, in the ordinary acceptation of the term, Mark Twain doesn't lecture at all. He rambles on with the set purpose of rambling. ... But Mark Twain can act and dramatise his points when he cares to or thinks it necessary."

Reviewing the third lecture, the *Herald* reported: "Mark Twain doesn't give you breathing space to take his good things up critically and examine them; but each time invites you to come along and listen to his next, which is always better than the one before. And this was probably the reason why the audience, which had shouted such a splendid welcome to him when he came upon the stage, was not a whit less demonstrative when he bowed himself out of sight."

He concluded his final lecture in Sydney with a poem based on names of Australian towns. "There are 81 in the

A SWELTERING DAY IN AUSTRALIA

"HELLO, MARK"

AFTER YOU, MARK TWAIN

list. I did not need them all, but I knocked down 66 of them, which is a good bag for a person not in the business. The best word on that list and the most musical and gurgly is Woolloomooloo. It is a place near Sydney. It has 8 o's in it."

A SWELTERING DAY IN AUSTRALIA
(To be read soft and low, with the lights turned down.)

The Bombola faints in the hot Bowral tree,
　　　　Where fierce Mullengudgery's smothering fires
Far from the breezes of Coolgardie
　　　　Burn ghastly and blue as the day expires;

And Murriwillumba complaineth in song
　　　　For the garlanded bowers of Woolloomooloo,
And the Ballarat Fly and the lone Wollongong
　　　　They dream of the gardens of Jamberoo;

The wallabi sighs for the Murrumbidgee,
　　　　For the velvety sod of the Munno Parah,
Where the waters of healing from Muloowurtie
　　　　Flow dim in the gloaming by Yaranyackah;

The Koppio sorrows for lost Wolloway,
　　　　And sigheth in secret for Murrurundi,
The Whangaroa wombat lamenteth the day
　　　　That made him an exile from Jerrilderie;

The Teawamute Tumut from Wirrega's glade,
　　　　The Nangkita swallow, the Wallaroo swan,
They long for the peace of the Timaru shade
　　　　And thy balmy soft airs, O sweet Mittagong!

The Kooringa buffalo pants in the sun,
　　　　The Kondoparinga lies gaping for breath,
The Kongorong Comaum to the shadow has won
　　　　But the Goomeroo sinks in the slumber of death.

60

A SWELTERING DAY IN AUSTRALIA

In the weltering hell of the Moorooroo plain
      The Yatala Wangary withers and dies,
And the Worrow Wanilla, demented with pain,
      To the Woolgoolga woodlands despairingly flies;

Sweet Nangwarry's desolate, Coonamble wails,
      And Tungkillo Kuitpo in sables is drest,
For the Whangarei winds fall asleep in the sails
      And the Booleroo life-breeze is dead in the west.

Myponga, Kapunda, O slumber no more!
      Yankalilla, Parawirra, be warned!
There's death in the air! Killanoola, wherefore
      Shall the prayer of Penola be scorned?

Cootamundra, and Takee, and Wakatipu,
      Toowoomba, Kaikoura are lost!
From Oukaparinga to far Oamaru
      All burn in this hell's holocaust!

Parramatta and Binnum are gone to their rest
      In the vale of Tapanni Taroom,
Kawakawa, Deniliquin—all that was best
      In the earth are but graves and a tomb!

Narrandera mourns, Cameroo answers not
      When the roll of the scathless we cry:
Tongariro, Goondiwindi, Woolundunga, the spot
      Is mute and forlorn where ye lie.

The *Herald* concluded its review: "Everyone went home on the best of terms with himself."

We were hungry for open spaces and big sky. The public bus from Sydney to Melbourne went through ranching country. The isolation was there. Houses with extended metal roofs huddled with outbuildings in clumps of trees. Red, sunbaked earth, broken only by occasional eroded coulees, constituted the pastureland. We felt the appeal of the country spreading endlessly in every direction, but where was the grass? Where, in fact, was the sky? The blue sky we had expected was here effused with a pink haze, which blurred the distant outlines of the horizon. That Australia was in the fourth year of its worst drought in history was evident.

We had noticed the thin, anemic trees, growing singly, in forests, or in clumps along the way. At our first tea stop, we learned that they are eucalyptus, called gums by the Aussies. The whole country smells of them, like camphor or witch hazel—astringent, aromatic, pungent, and clean. The air is dry and bracing like that of our high-country plains, where the aroma is of sagebrush and pine. It seems more than an odor that emanates from the gums; more like a vapour, which mixes with the pink dust, giving it body and pasting it on the sky.

In this sunburned country the gum is known as the tree that gives no shade. It seems an almost inexcusable fault in a tree. Its leaves hang vertically! Cattle, which on the Montana range seek the shelter of pine and cottonwood, ignored the sparse shade afforded by the gum trees and stood listlessly in the sunshine. Yet in the absence of other vegetation, the eucalyptus is king. Consider its qualifications: there are more than four hundred species from scrub bushes to trees the height of redwoods, all native to Australia.

Like us, Mark Twain was fascinated by these trees. "Great melancholy gum trees, with trunks rugged with curled sheets of flaking bark—erysipelas convalescents, so to speak, shedding their dead skins. ... Those sad gums stood up out of the dry white clay, pictures of patience and resignation. It is a tree that can get along without water; still it is fond of it—ravenously so. It is a very intelligent tree and will detect the presence of hidden water at a distance of fifty feet, and send out slender long root-fibres to prospect it."

The fact that koalas, which have become Australia's symbol, eat nothing but eucalyptus leaves, does not reflect much glory on the country. Scientists have recently discovered that a chemical in the leaves affects koalas much as marijuana affects humans, which may explain why these dopey creatures are rather crochety and not nearly as cute as in the Quantas ads.

This was the country of the bushrangers, as famous in Australia—and as sympathetically portrayed—as the Daltons and the James brothers of the American West. Natural spin-offs from the penal colonies, they were originally escaped convicts who took up cattle rustling. The end of the Kelly gang, the last of the bushrangers, came in a shootout in 1880.

We passed the town of Wagga-Wagga, "the place of black crows." It was named by the Aborigines, who, having no plurals in their language, simply said the word twice. Midway between Sydney and Melbourne, we lunched in the capital city of Canberra, a sterile planned city built after Australia achieved dominion status in the British Commonwealth of Nations in 1901. The Victorian Alps, said to offer the best skiing in Australia, loomed briefly off to the southeast.

Melbourne, the capital of the state of Victoria, prides itself that it was not settled by convicts and that it was the center for the country's richest and most prolonged gold rush. In 1851, two years after the great gold rush in California, gold seekers sought their El Dorado in southern Australia. Mark Twain reported:

A hundred thousand people poured into Melbourne from England and other countries in a single month,

and flocked away to the mines. The crews of the
ships that brought them flocked with them; the clerks
in the government offices followed; so did the cooks,
the maids, the coachmen, the butlers, and the other
domestic servants; so did the carpenters, the smiths,
the plumbers, the painters, the reporters, the editors, the lawyers, the clients, the barkeepers, the
bummers, the blacklegs, the thieves, the loose
women, the grocers, the butchers, the bakers, the
doctors, the druggists, the nurses; so did the police;
even officials of high and hitherto envied place threw
up their positions and joined the procession.

In ten years the population of the area had tripled
and surface mining was finished. But much of this vast
and ambitious labor pool remained to pioneer the new
continent. The trouble was that now there weren't enough
jobs to go around. The new immigrants turned their
attention to the land, but in the mining states of Victoria
and New South Wales, the squatters were there before
them. Mark Twain explains: "With us, when you speak of
a squatter you are ... speaking of a poor man, but in
Australia when you speak of a squatter you are ... speaking
of a millionaire; in America the word indicates the pos-
sessor of a few acres and a doubtful title, in Australia it
indicates a man whose land front is as long as a railroad
... in America if your uncle is a squatter you keep it dark,
in Australia you advertise it."

Almost ten years of political fighting ensued before a
land reform measure comparable to the U.S. Homestead
Act was passed, allowing potential farmers to select land
from squatters' runs. As in the American West, however,
the squatters had farsightedly picked out the water holes,
creeks, and best pastures, and in some cases, bought
parcels on behalf of family members, friends, or imaginary
persons.

Instead of proving up on a homestead, as in the West,
Australians moved onto their "selection." More than two

A SWELTERING DAY IN AUSTRALIA

million Australians have seen the play *On Our Selection,* which has been a hit since 1912. We recognized our homesteader ancestors in the family of Dad Rudd in a hilarious production by the Melbourne Theatre Company. The hit of the play was an aged black Labrador which scratched on cue.

Melbourne claims to be the financial, fashion, food, and cultural center of Australia. It is undoubtedly cosmopolitan. I picked up a tourist brochure advertising escort services, featuring such names as Shady Lady, Oriental Delights, Executive Escorts (sensuous and extremely friendly, but not inexpensive), Goodtime Girls, and Wineglow ("our ladies, like wine, mature with age and experience"). There was one escort service for women— a shopping tour.

This city proclaims a general public holiday for a horse race—the Melbourne Cup. Emulating Ascot in England, the event calls for formal attire and hats. Since it is not possible to put on the dog in Australia with a completely straight face, the irreverent young have taken to showing up in outlandish costumes and spoofs of evening dress, giving the affair something of a Mardi Gras effect. The Aussies claim it is the biggest cocktail party in the world. In the United States it would be a tailgate party.

Although said to be the most British city in Australia, Melbourne is actually the Australian melting pot. Half its population was either born overseas or had a parent born overseas. Melbourne has the third largest Greek population in the world, after Athens and Salonica, and has the Greek restaurants to prove it. But the American influence is insidious and pervasive. The television schedule included *The Partridge Family, Alias Smith and Jones, Diff'rent Strokes, Bewitched, Sesame Street, Here's Lucy, Hawaii Five-O, Richard Simmons, Hogan's Heroes, M*A*S*H, The Waltons, Candid Camera,* and *The Odd Couple.* A high

school band in the mall near Meyer's, which claims to be
the largest department store in the southern hemisphere,
was playing a holiday concert: "Everything's Up-to-date
in Kansas City" and "Deep in the Heart of Texas."

We felt very much at home in Melbourne. As we were
eating at a pub on Little Collins Street on New Year's Eve,
we were invited to join a nearby couple and ended up as
their guests on a guided tour of the city, across the harbor
bridge (a span of which collapsed during construction in
1970, killing thirty-seven men), and to their home in the
suburb of Williamstown. During the evening our host
never referred to the British as anything but "the bloody
poms." Australians do not seem to share the New
Zealanders' attachment to England. Yet when we were
there, Australia's national anthem was "God Save the
Queen."

Our hosts dropped us off near our hotel shortly
before midnight. We made our way through throngs of
noisy, celebrating young people, many of whom wished us
a happy New Year. Although police were in evidence, the
mood was merely exuberant. At midnight there was a
magnificent hullabaloo, which continued until dawn. It
had been years since we had witnessed such a cordial
welcome to a new year. What would have happened, we
reflected, if we'd been dropped off under similar circumstances
in an American inner city on New Year's Eve?

On New Year's Day we tackled the eleven-hour bus
ride from Melbourne to Adelaide. Between Melbourne
and Ballarat we drove along a fifteen-mile avenue of trees
called the Road of Remembrance. Each tree bears the
name of an Australian soldier who died in World War I.
It was a simple and compelling memorial. Australia's
monuments differ in both style and content from those of
the Kiwis.

CHAPTER V

Back to Bangladesh

My Golden Bengal, I love you,
O mother, whatever wealth this poor man has,
    I place before your feet.
O mother, no more shall I buy
    in the houses of others
    this so-called finery of yours
a noose around my neck.

Rabindranath Tagore, Bengali poet
National anthem of Bangladesh

Siam (Thailand) was never a British colony, although both the British and the French tried, while adventuring in Indochina, to insert themselves by either arms or trade. Since there was no large English-speaking audience, Mark Twain did not lecture here. But it was en route to Bangladesh, which was part of India in Twain's day, so we stopped in Bangkok.

Earlier we had stayed at the Erewohn Hotel, a bastion of early European influence and elegance—a shaded, shuttered and quiet hostelry of solid mahogany, teak, ceiling fans, bidets, and deferential staff. It was sufficiently exotic for us. But well-travelled friends said, "You owe it to yourselves to stay at the Oriental—the best hotel in the world." Had not Joseph Conrad stayed at this historic hotel ("In the light of the crimson sunset all ablaze behind the golden pagodas, I made my way to the Oriental,"

A CAB SUBSTITUTE

wrote Conrad) as well as Somerset Maugham, James Michener and Noel Coward? All have suites named after them in the Authors' Wing.

After our long drive from the airport past flooded rice paddies and ponds where small boys tended or slept on the backs of water buffalo, the clamor of metropolitan Bangkok seemed inappropriate. Here was our first experience in Asiatic gridlock, a traffic maze which far outstrips that of any western city. It consists of the intricate interweaving of burdened pedestrians, baby taxis (similar to golf carts), bicycles, handcarts, buses, and automobiles, under a cacophonous pall of air and noise pollution.

The approach to the Oriental was anything but pre-possessing. It was simply a wide porte cochere at the end of a narrow and twisting alleyway. But it was flanked by a squadron of attendants costumed for *The King and I*. A small, smiling boy bowed as he opened the door to the lobby. Did I say lobby? It was like no hotel lobby on this earth. It gleamed. It had the hushed, sanctified aura of a cathedral. The chandeliers hanging from the remote ceiling were clumps of giant temple bells with gold filigree clappers.

A wall of windows overlooked the swimming pool and framed the nearby Chao Phraya River and slowly drifting sampans silhouetted against the sunset. Arrangements of orchids met the eye at unexpected niches in hallways, bordering a marble fountain, on the grand piano in the Authors' Lounge, and appeared in our room along with a basket of fruit too beautiful to eat, a gift of Kurt Wachtveitl, the Swiss general manager of the hotel. He had come to the Oriental after training at the Lake Lausanne School for Hotel Management and after having worked in St. Moritz, London and the Mandarin International in Hong Kong, said to be the second-ranking of the world's hostelries.

A beautiful young Thai woman costumed in iridescent

silk patrolled the lobby, dumping ashtrays and discreetly
polishing fingerprints from glass-topped tables the moment
guests arose. Almost a thousand people, nearly all Thais,
are employed by the Oriental, and Kurt Wachtveitl says
it is a pleasure to work with them. "We train them for one
month and you see them. They are, by nature, a very
gracious people, anxious to please."

Relaxing after our long flight, we were surprised that
tea-making facilities, to which we had grown accustomed
in New Zealand and Australia, were not in the room.
When we called the desk, our tea arrived in half an hour,
brewing in a lovely china pot (with cozy). It cost five
dollars, plus tip. We discovered, sipping gin and tonics
(four dollars each) on the River Terrace, that the primary
patrons of the Oriental are executive travellers on expense accounts. The price for a night there is two hundred
dollars, minimum. Our room was truly beautiful and luxuri-
ous. Bangkok visitors without expense accounts should stay at
the Erewohn and visit the lobby of the Oriental.

The tour of the royal palace grounds was eye-boggling:
red- and green-tiled roofs, temple spires, and fanciful
figures of animals and mythical beings. Everything had
been newly gilded or painted for Thailand's bicentennial
festivities. The whole marvelous place glittered, more
spectacular than Disneyland and more distinguished for
its antiquity. But to savor Thailand's tranquility and
beauty in earnest, we were taken by Noi Vilawan, who had
been an American Field Service student in our hometown
of Bigfork, Montana, to "the ancient city" an hour's drive
outside Bangkok. Originally the site of the summer palace
of Siamese kings, it is now a showcase of architecturally
significant buildings, collected from all over Thailand by
a wealthy businessman and transported here for preser-
vation and display.

BACK TO BANGLADESH

Elegant rooms with gleaming teak floors and elaborately ornamented walls of gilded lacquer work, chronicling state ceremonies of centuries past, stand there for inspection, unguarded, in a peaceful setting of palm trees and ponds. The palace rooms are furnished with simple elegance—beautifully carved chests and low benches, boxes and religious objects. Ancient Hindu and Buddhist temples are there in all their gorgeous flamboyance. The Temple of the Buddha's Footprint is approached up long stairways with bannisters of stone dragons. There is an unhurried, reverent, tropical charm about the immense compound. We were the only visitors.

After so much splendid viewing, we were treated to a view of Thais at home—dinner with Noi's extended family in Bangkok. One of twelve children, she lives with her brother, three sisters, four nephews and three nieces, according to our count. Her mother is not living and her father lives in another city. Noi and her brother attend the nearby university where Noi is in law school. (She received an award from King Bhumibol for having the highest grade in the law school entrance examination. We saw a photo of the presentation.)

The three sisters prepared and served an elaborate, delicious meal. They care for the swarm of children who belong to various brothers and sisters of the family who live and work outside Bangkok. The children are sent into the city to attend private schools and receive a quality education.

A large square building on a quiet street, the house was comfortable and attractive, well suited to the activities and needs of the children, who shyly demonstrated their best manners in greeting us, helped serve the many spicy dishes, ate their dinner at a separate table, and retired to watch television or do homework. It seemed a lively, happy family with the sisters in complete command. Much

71

has been lost in our country with the demise of multi-generational living and live-in aunts.

Although our plane for Dhaka left early the next morning, Noi, her brother, and her university friends insisted on taking us to the airport. Up to this point, airports had been sedate and orderly. But in Bangkok airport the Indian subcontinent begins. Bangladesh-bound Bengalis were loading up in an atmosphere of excitement, stress, panic. Greetings and farewells were emotional and vocal. Children, gotten up in their best clothes to look like miniature adults, chased each other around family groups and played on the floor. People juggled carry-on bundles of plastic shopping bags and bulging, handmade baskets crammed with radios, tape recorders, and appliances.

The few white passengers were not tourists or business travellers with briefcases, but development aid types bound for Bangladesh to work on the many projects which have sprung up in the wake of Bengal's hurricanes, wars, and famines, or returning to Dhaka, the capital, after leave.

Two bearded Sikhs, not deigning to stoop to the emotionalism of the Bengalis, bade stately farewells to three similarly bearded Sikhs. All wore immaculately tailored business suits. Each was splendidly, radiantly, turbanned. A procession of a dozen saffron-robed Buddhist monks was shepherded up the aisle of the airplane and assigned seats by a "brother superior" wearing spectacles and carrying a clipboard.

"Where are they going?" we asked the flight attendant, since we couldn't recall ever having seen a Buddhist monastery in Muslim Dhaka.

"To Chittagong," she answered. Ah, yes, Chittagong, at the very tip of Bangladesh, on the Bay of Bengal and near the border of Burma.

BACK TO BANGLADESH

As noon approached, the brother superior conferred urgently with the flight steward. Buddhist monks may not take food after noon. There was much scurrying in the flight kitchen. Soon trays were served to the monks. Surreptitiously we watched two middle-aged celibates across the aisle as they tackled their plastic-packaged airline fare. After conferring, they carefully peeled off the wrappings. We thought we detected a giggle. Whether or not they had ever tasted such food before, they ate it with relish.

The youngest neophyte steered a feeble old monk down the aisle to the toilet several times during the flight. The face of the frail patriarch and the round, almost babyish face of the youth, each rising from the orange anonymity of his robe, is a *National Geographic* photo engraved on memory.

It had begun. We were flying above the Indian subcontinent where life is not like that in any other part of the world. From now on our senses would be challenged by the alien, the exotic, the wonderful. Looking down, the earth was a green crazy quilt of rice paddies, meandering rivers, forests of palm trees, and tiny dots of bamboo huts on earthen embankments.

Dhaka airport is no longer the warehouse-like structure we had known when we arrived there twenty years before for a two-year stay. The city had grown from 0.5 million to 3.5 million, covering more than fifty-six square miles. The airport had been moved out to the old army cantonment where U.S. pilots landed if they were lucky enough to make it over the "Burma hump" in World War II.

Hanan, now head of the Ford Foundation office in Dhaka and a former associate of Winston's, met the plane. So did Abu, our old driver. It was an emotional reunion. They had been our friends and helpers, easing our adjustment to living in a city and country completely foreign to us. Hanan had arranged the furnishing and employed servants for our comfortable new home. Hanan and the Ford Foundation staff had enabled Winston to function in his job as advisor in administration to head-masters in twenty-one pilot high schools scattered throughout what was then East Pakistan. Abu had driven Winston safely over hundreds of miles of often dangerous roads, to ferries and boats and helicopters to the remote schools. And Abu had driven me to my job as a secretary at the cholera research laboratory and hospital on the outskirts of Dhaka, and enabled me to explore the exotic bazaars and markets in the old city.

We were given use of quarters at the Ford Foundation staff flat, a facility normally reserved for travellers on project-related business; it was a much appreciated courtesy. Winston vanished onto the campus of the Education Extension Centre where he had been headquartered, for joyful meetings with his long-ago counterpart, Mrs. Quazi Jahan Khan, and other old friends and co-workers. In the days that followed he was to learn all too frequently of the sad fate of headmasters and teachers at schools he had helped establish. Under the aegis of the University of Chicago and the Ford Foundation, as well as the East Pakistan government, the schools were designed to introduce comprehensive, American-type education in business, science, crafts, home economics, and agriculture to aug-ment the British system. Because of their success, the schools became particular targets for attack by the West Pakistan army when it invaded in 1972.

The Bay of Bengal is the ultimate fruit of the subcontinent. Into it the great rivers of India, which dwarf the Missis-sippi and are equalled only by the Amazon, pour the makings of the delta that is Bangladesh. The meandering lower reaches of the Ganges, the Meghna, and the Brahmaputra have deposited here one great, wide plain, low-lying and fertile.

Dhaka (formerly Dacca), the capital, is the central market for this vast farmland. Although its remoteness and the stunning heat and humidity that prevail for half the year earned it a reputation as a punishment post among the British, it has for centuries been a cosmopolitan center for trade in rice, indigo, salt, betel nut, pink pearls, jute, and fine cotton cloth. In spite of recent highrise office buildings and luxury hotels, Dhaka remains relatively untouched by foreign influences. In fact, East Bengal, as it was called when it was part of India and before it became East Pakistan and finally Bangladesh, remained relatively untouched by conquerors since the time of Alexander the Great. Strange ideas and foreign blood never contaminated its isolated, uniquely Indian culture.

The Bengalis have always marched to a different drummer. The rhythm of their days is ordained by the seasons and the caprice of the river. Music, poetry, classical dance, and conversation are Bengali talents. The British found the Bengalis indifferent soldiers—although they fought fiercely when East Pakistan was invaded by their fellow Muslims from West Pakistan in 1971 in a vengeful rampage. Helped by India, East Pakistan became the independent state of Bangladesh in 1972.

Now we were in Muslim country. For the first time on our journey we heard the voices of muezzins from the minarets of mosques at dawn, noon, and sundown, reciting the prayer of Islam: "I praise the perfection of Allah, the Forever existing; the perfection of Allah, the Desired, the Existing, the Single, the Supreme; the perfection of Allah, the One, the Sole ... " as devout Muslims faced Mecca to pray. Public address systems installed in minarets have augmented the decibels but diminished the haunting appeal of the invocation.

Bangladesh has more than seventy-five million people squeezed into an area the size of Alabama. Its population density of 1,500 per square mile makes it the most densely settled developing country. One hundred years ago the birth rate was forty-five to fifty live births per thousand and the death rate was forty to forty-five per thousand. Famines and epidemics acted as a brake on population growth. Today, with the birth rate substantially unchanged, and the death rate down to about twenty per thousand thanks to inoculations, sanitation, and better health care and nutrition, the population is growing so fast that it will probably double by the twenty-first century. Almost half of the people are younger than fifteen. While family planning has been introduced, babies continue to be the crop that never fails. Half of all "women" are married by age thirteen and nearly all are married by nineteen. The average family size in the 1961 census was 5.6.

Visualize, if you can, that only 4 percent of all these millions are living away from their birthplaces and that only 6 percent live in urban centers, and you realize how truly rural this land is. Some 94 percent of the people live in the more than sixty-five thousand villages. As far as women are concerned, consider the fact that not only have most of them never been outside their village, but most have never even been outside their home courtyard. Only 8 percent of the people are functionally literate (five or more years of school).

In Dhaka the hot, brilliant colors of the tropics assault the eye—the flamboyant blossoms of overarching trees, the lush green of paddy fields and bamboo groves stretching in all directions from the city, still life market arrangements of tomatoes, cauliflower, pineapple, clay pots, bananas. The thousand-hued saris of women are

" From Greenland's icy mountains,
From India's coral strand,
Where Afric's sunny fountains
Roll down their golden sand.
From many an ancient river,
From many a palmy plain,
They call us to deliver
Their land from error's chain."

proudly displayed since the black burkah covering mandated by fundamentalist Shiite Muslims was abandoned during the war of liberation. Wildly decorated rickshaws and trucks abound; men turbanned and breeched in brilliant purple, red, and green push handcarts, carry burdens on their heads, or row riverboats—on every street, in every lane, on every river, life pulsates and commerce flourishes.

To come to Bangladesh is to step back in time to the days of Mohammed; to erase the industrial revolution and view a people whose every possession is handmade by themselves or their neighbors.

Overwhelmed by its strangeness, its size, its vast and varying populations, its unaccustomed climate, fearful of its strange diseases, travellers hesitate to tackle India and Bangladesh on their own. But it is not possible to get an inkling of what it's all about from a packaged tour. It is simply necessary to go there and plunge in.

AFTER YOU, MARK TWAIN

We knew that the war of liberation had devastated the family of my friend, Shahana (not her real name). Her husband is dead. She and her sons, we learned, were living as refugees. I had met Shahana at the Dacca Club, a musty relic of the British Raj, with the only grass courts I've played tennis on in my entire life. Shahana was not only playing tennis in that land of *purdah* (the seclusion of women) and the *burkah* (the veil)—she was playing tennis in slacks! We played frequently and often she came home with me for lemonade (without ice, for no matter how hot the day, Bengalis have a horror of chilling the stomach).

We were once invited to spend a holiday at her home outside the city. There, at an old mansion built by the Dutch East India Company in the last century as headquarters for an indigo plantation, the beautiful Shahana told me what it meant to be an Indian woman. That night I wrote it down just as she had told it to me.

Shahana's mother died at nineteen when Shahana was four. There were two younger sisters. Death at an early age was a fact of life for women in Bengal, and her widowed father was soon remarried to an illiterate woman chosen by his family. The three sisters were cared for by ayahs (nursemaids) and sent to a Catholic boarding school in Darjeeling. There Shahana made friends with British girls, excelled in sports, and graduated at the head of her class when she was fifteen. She then returned home to Dacca.

"Home? I had no home. I had no friends. There was nothing to do. Women in this country do nothing. I was so lonely. The days simply passed. I spent hours on the roof of the house watching the people on the street and envying them. Do you understand that I have never in all my life gone out of the house alone? Not even to go shopping or visiting or for a drive. And when I did go out, I was covered with a burkah."

BACK TO BANGLADESH

One day her stepmother announced that her father had decided it was time for her to marry. Was she willing? Shahana knew nothing of marriage or of men. She had never spoken with a man other than her father. She finally agreed to be married since anything would be an improvement on her lonely life.

"All I knew of my bridegroom was that he was of good family and that he had been graduated from Cambridge University in the United Kingdom.

"Daddy began to select my trousseau, as is the custom. Women do not go to the market. A bride must have clothes for a year, and a different sari for every day. Saris came by the dozens, each one more beautiful, with the most important the red silk wedding sari woven with gold. My stepmother did not approve. It was too expensive.

"It was really quite laughable that I did not know how to wrap a sari. I had never worn one. Most upper-class girls wear the *shalwar* chemise (a fitted shift over loose trousers) and at school I had worn a uniform. But most Bengali girls grow up with women and know how to wrap a sari. I had to learn then.

"The gifts of clothes and jewelry from the bridegroom's family arrived, as is the custom. The jewelry was of gold set with diamonds—so heavy, so ornate. The *montika* (golden ornament) for the forehead was so very large— and the earrings—down to here!

"It was then that they noticed that my ears were not pierced. I had never worn jewelry. Here all girls, no matter how poor, have their ears pierced when they are babies. But nobody had thought to pierce my ears; nor, of course, had I. But it was unthinkable that I should not wear the gifts of my husband's family. So my ears were pierced three days before the wedding.

"The wedding festivities last three days. On the day when the bridegroom's family comes to the bride's house,

79

they ask for her consent. I was seated and told to keep my eyes cast down and to appear shy and sad. This was not hard to do. But once I stole a glance at my future husband. He seemed very old.

"Later he told me that when he saw me he was shocked that I was so young and so small—nothing but a child.

"That night my old *ayah* came to me and told me that she would go with me the next day to my husband's house. 'You must be brave. It is for a woman to be brave.'

"She did not tell me for what I was to be brave. I had no idea. I knew that something was supposed to happen, but I did not know what it was.

"On the day of the wedding the women dressed me in many petticoats and the red wedding sari. My hands and feet were stained with henna. Everything according to custom. The problem was that I did not understand the custom. I knew better the Christian custom, although I had never attended a Catholic wedding either.

"The vows were read. The Imam recited the verses from the Holy Koran. My husband and I looked at each other's faces in a mirror underneath a veil. Then we separated for the wedding feast, he to eat with the men and I with the women, as is the custom.

"It was late at night when we were led to the bedroom. I was exhausted. The room and bed were beautifully decorated with flowers and paper cut-outs of good wishes in Bengali script.

"For the first time I was alone with a man. I was apprehensive. But I had made up my mind to be brave. Something bad was going to happen and I wanted to get it over with. I belonged to this man. I would live in his house. I was not sad at leaving my home.

"We stood facing each other in the big bedroom. He said nothing. He simply stood and looked at me until I was most embarrassed and wondered if he found me ugly. I, too, looked at him. For I was curious.

"It was not what you westerners call 'love at first sight.' He seemed very old to me. He was twenty-seven. When you are fifteen, twenty-seven seems very old indeed. This, too, is the custom. He was not handsome. But his face was noble and his eyes were kind. Suddenly I was no longer afraid.

" 'Please sit down,' he said at last. He brought a chair and sat facing me. 'I want to talk to you. ... Are you afraid?'

" 'Yes,' I answered. Then, 'No... I was afraid. But now, suddenly, I am no longer afraid.'

" 'Good,' he said. 'You do not need to be afraid. Now tell me, what things do you like to do?'

"So I told him of my school and my love for reading and sports and riding, how I wanted to learn more and to continue my education. I told him about the books I liked and about my friends at the sisters' school who had now gone home to Europe to live. It was so good to have somebody to talk to after the lonely months. I told him about my stepmother and how miserable my life had been at home.

"Then I felt a hand on my shoulder. It was my *ayah*, who whispered in my ear, 'You talk too much. Act modest and afraid. Your actions are a disgrace. No wonder your husband is acting so strangely.'

"For the first time I looked about and realized that eyes were peering in the doors and windows. I blushed with shame that my conduct had been inappropriate.

"My husband rose and then I became afraid. Such a rage! He shouted to my *ayah*. 'Get out!' Striding to the door he drove away the onlookers with a fury I have not seen in the twenty years we have now been married. When he came back to the chair he was pale and trembling. 'Barbarians!' he said.

" 'Now what were we talking about?' he began. But

the spell was broken. Realizing that I had somehow acted incorrectly, I wept.

" 'Never mind, child,' he said, taking my hand. 'Whatever the *ayah* said was not right. From today I will tell you, not your *ayah*, not anyone, not even your father. ... Now, make yourself comfortable. Take off that heavy jewelry. You look like you have a weight on your head.'

"I tried to remove the necklace, but the clasp was unfamiliar. He unfastened it for me and then lifted the *montika* from my head. Then he knelt and gently removed the torturous earrings, the weight of which, pulling my inflamed earlobes was so terribly painful. I could not help crying out as he removed them.

"Without a word, he put the jewelry on the dressing table. When he again faced me I could see that he was once more angry. 'When did they pierce your ears?' he asked.

" 'It's been three days now,' I explained. 'It had to be done because of the custom.'

" 'The hell with the custom,' he roared, and gathering me in his arms, he rocked me like a child. 'Poor baby!' he said. 'Poor child. But now you do not have to worry. Now I will take care of you. Nobody will hurt you again.'

"It seemed most natural for him to help me remove the beautiful sari. Together we folded its six-yard length and laid it carefully in a drawer along with the many petticoats. I covered myself with my nightdress. He carried me to the bed and tucked me in like a child, then called a bearer to bring a basin of water, towels and tea.

"Like a nurse, he sponged my face and cleansed my poor ears. Then he propped me up in the big bed and we drank tea.

"Finally he asked, 'Do you know what it is to be married?'

" 'No,' I confessed. 'I know that something bad is going to happen and that I must be brave.'

BACK TO BANGLADESH

"My husband is not a profane man, but he swore. Then he said, 'Now listen to me, child. Nothing bad is going to happen to you. Tomorrow I will bring you a book which will explain everything to you. We will read the book together and if you have any questions, please ask me. Now we are both tired and we will go to sleep.'

"He put out the light and soon he crept in beside me and took my hand and we slept.

"Ah, God was good to me! But how many such men are there in this land? My sisters have told me. I tried to prepare them, but how can you prepare a girl to be raped by a stranger? My sisters have told me how it was. And for a woman it can never be good afterward. God help them! Thank God I have only sons."

Malnutrition and tropical diseases are widespread in Bangladesh. In the 1960s a cholera research laboratory, now known as the International Centre for Diarrhoeal Disease Research, was established. Dhaka was chosen because cholera can almost always be found here. I worked at the cholera center briefly during our two-year stay.

Sister Dorothy Torrance, a capable, no-nonsense British nurse who commanded the attached hospital, introduced me to the disease and its treatment. Patients lay on cots covered with plastic sheets. At the center of the sheet, a plastic funnel and tube led to a bucket underneath the bed, on which were marked metric liquid measurements. Amounts of lost body fluids were checked at regular intervals, and glucose/saline solution equal to the fluid loss was replaced in the patient intravenously. The problems associated with this precise treatment in the villages of Bangladesh can well be imagined, of which the necessity for sterile techniques was only one.

We learned about today's improved oral rehydration therapy (ORT) from Dr. Jeff Harris and Dr. Mary

Chamberland, both associated with the Center for Disease Control, Atlanta, and both doing research at the Dhaka laboratory. The glucose/saline has now been packaged into ten-cent sachets which, when dissolved in boiled water and drunk, replace the liquids and salts lost in cholera and similar illnesses.

The conventional wisdom in the Peace Corps for survival in India is: "If you can't cook it, peel it, or boil it, forget it." Like many tourists to the region, we had provided ourselves with a diarrhea preventive antibiotic, which we planned to begin taking when uncertain about the safety of our food and drink. The advice of the two doctors, however, was: "Don't use it. It will do more harm than good. Be careful of what you eat and drink. If you do contract a diarrhea which is severe or persists for more than two days, get ORT from a pharmacy. Drink as much of this as you need until the symptoms end." We proceeded through India and Sri Lanka with no symptoms whatsoever.

I found Khushi Kabir on the second floor of a house on a quiet residential street. This daughter of a prominent Bengali family emerged from the liberation war as a leader of women. Handsome and forthright, she described the anger of the time in the early 1970s when the repression of the Bengalis by West Pakistan precipitated the uprising in which it is estimated a million people died. An art student at Dacca University, she joined in parading and singing the revolutionary songs which were outlawed by the West Pakistan occupation forces. Such conduct by a woman in this Muslim society was almost unheard of. Today the poised, confident Khushi Kabir heads up a program of her own devising to benefit the landless poor of Bangladesh. The project is called *Nijera Kori*, meaning "We do it ourselves."

She admits, "I had to push myself into doing something. Because of my class and because I was a woman, many felt very strongly that it was not a good idea for me to go to the villages to work for women. But I went to a village in 1974. It worked very well. The men accepted me—or I assume they accepted me, because there was no reaction. I was the only woman working in the area with a hundred men. There was one program for women at Jamalpur and one at Syhlet.

"In our village there were programs in literacy and health for men, but none for women. It was very difficult to get educated women to help. We started recruiting them from Dhaka. Women had never gone out to work and, in fact, had never gone outside their homes. It was a whole new kind of behavior. Today women have jobs in business, airlines, and so on, but it is still very difficult to get as many women as we would like to work in the villages. But this is changing. We now have a ratio of forty-six women to fifty-four men in our organization.

"What we are doing is helping both women and men to form their own organizations. Co-ops have so many rules and laws that we don't really go in for them. We have an informal co-op. Our aim is to claim for the landless poor newly reclaimed fallow land owned by the government. There is much new land created every year by the changing channels of the rivers. There is lots of red tape involved. We encourage a group to get together to stand up for themselves. They save money and use it collectively and use the land collectively as well. When somebody is in distress, money can be lent to them.

"Desertion of women has greatly increased since the war. Deserted women are now permitted to remarry, but it is difficult for them to live and support their children in the meantime. There are very few jobs in a village. Now the women are getting together and they are being heard in the village councils for the first time. They are protesting against corruption. They get up and make the men listen. They say, 'Listen, you can't kick us around any more.' Surprisingly, a lot of the men's groups are very support-ive of the women. We have started organizing a network of women from other agencies. We know which women are organizers and we know what's going on. We call this network *Nari Pokkho*, which means, 'on the side of women.'

"One man told me recently, 'Talking to you is like talking to another man.' I regard that as a compliment. That does not mean that I have to become a man to do something important. We can be women and be capable." In this world of arranged marriages, the attractive Khushi had married a man of her own choosing, a fellow worker in *Nijera Kori*.

Important work on women's programs has been done by Martha Alter Chen, who planned and administered a program for impoverished village women under the Bangladesh Rural Advancement Committee (BRAC), a long-term project supported by Oxfam-America. Marty Chen, the organization's field representative for India and Bangladesh, is the daughter of missionaries, and fluent in Hindi and Bengali. She has lived on the subcontinent for most of her life.

She points out that development programs are usu-ally directed toward men, and women-oriented programs generally focus on women's reproductive roles, to the neglect of their productive roles. Most property is held in men's names, which results in women having little access to capital and income; having fewer skills and less literacy than men; and working at lower pay in the most menial of jobs. At the same time, they work what is termed the "double day"—collecting fuel, fodder, and water; processing and cooking food; caring for children; washing clothes; and cleaning homes in addition to their jobs.

BACK TO BANGLADESH

It is generally agreed that the only long-term solution to the persistent and growing problem of hunger in the world is increasing the productivity and incomes of those whose lives are most directly involved—the small farmers and landless poor. Borrowing as little as ten or twenty dollars can enable a poor farmer to buy livestock or start a food-processing enterprise. The loan rate recovery from such programs is almost 100 percent. Assistance for such programs in developing countries is both cheaper and more useful than expenditures on steel mills or military hardware, for example. War is a luxury that developing countries cannot afford.

Most Americans, and certainly the British, if we are to believe the characterizations in *The Jewel in the Crown*, *A Passage to India*, and countless reports from the time of the Raj, approach the subcontinent and its people with predisposed superiority. Never having the opportunity for a conversation with a scholar, an intellectual, or any individual not a rug wallah, hotel clerk, or beggar, tourists tend to leave with their prejudices confirmed. We were more fortunate.

Our last evening in Dacca was spent with the family of Dr. and Mrs. Abdullah Al-Muti Sharafuddin. It would be hard to imagine a more attractive and entertaining contingent. They speak precise English, with less of a British accent than most because they lived in the United States while Dr. Sharafuddin earned a doctorate in chemistry from the University of Chicago. A highly respected scientist and prominent in the Bangladesh government, he was formerly an associate of Winston's in the education center. They have remained fast friends.

It was fun to hear the family bantering about the hundreds of guests at the recent wedding of their daughter, a real Bengali beauty, and estimates of the number of saris and the accumulation of jewels with which she had been presented. She was just completing a master's degree in chemistry at Dhaka University. Not so much fun was hearing accounts of the family being pinned down in the crossfire of the war, and of the destruction of pilot high schools and the vicious slaughter of teachers and headmasters by the invading army. Contemplation of the future for Bangladesh, and the compelling need for literacy and sound educational policy, was the ongoing subject of the evening. We bade them a reluctant goodbye, wondering when we would meet again and feeling that we had barely begun our conversation.

CHAPTER VI

British Pomp
and Indian Color

There is only one India! It is the only country
that has a monopoly of grand and imposing specialties.
When another country has a remarkable thing, it
cannot have it all to itself—some other country has
a duplicate. But India—that is different. Its marvels
are its own; the patents cannot be infringed; imita-
tions are not possible. And think of the size of them,
the majesty of them, the weird and outlandish
character of the most of them!

Mark Twain

R udyard Kipling thought it was good for everyone
to see some little of the great Indian Empire and the
strange folk who move about it." Mark Twain wrote
to him with plans to do just that.

Dear Kipling:
Years ago you came from India to Elmira to
visit me. It has always been my purpose to return
that visit and that great compliment some day. I
shall arrive next January and you must be ready. I
shall come riding my ayah with his tusks adorned
with silver bells and ribbons and escorted by a troop
of native howdahs richly clad and mounted upon a
herd of wild bungalows; and you must be on hand
with a few bottles of ghee, for I shall be thirsty.

Kipling was not on hand to welcome us to India.
Instead we were greeted by a riot. AGITATION AND PARALYSIS

AFTER YOU, MARK TWAIN

STRIKE CALCUTTA was the headline in the *Calcutta Statesman* for Wednesday, January 18, 1984: "Shopowners have downed their shutters and panic grips the city. ... Demonstrators smashed the windscreens of private cars and slashed the tyres. Buses, trucks, and cars stood at awkward angles on major roads. ... Tram services were affected throughout the city. ... Taxi drivers charged exorbitant fares, especially between the city and the airport."

As our plane circled Calcutta's DumDum Airport a blood-red pall of polluted air caught the last rays of the sunset and sent crimson sparks flashing off the Hooghly River. It was an inauspicious arrival at a storied city. There were neither buses nor taxis in sight as we stood uncertainly at the gate of the deserted terminal, watching the sunset fade. After an argument with a uniformed official, and the transfer of substantial baksheesh, Winston was able to find an ancient cab with a fearful driver. The fare was indeed exorbitant, but we were grateful for transportation.

The twelve-mile drive along back roads and side alleys, past cardboard *bustees* (shacks), dodging chanting, torch-carrying processions and burned out buses, was the stuff of television news reports. Noise, smoke, confusion, glimpses of frenzied faces, men carrying *lathis* (clubs) and placards, chanting and shouting—alongside, evening meals were being cooked over open fires before hovels where life was proceeding as usual—made ours a memorable entrance to India's largest city.

The Fairlawn Hotel lay behind a wall on a shabby street. The iron gate was opened by an aged, red-turbanned *chowkidar* (watchman) to reveal a courtyard of greenery, colored lights, umbrellas, and tables. "India, A Travel Survival Kit" describes it: "A piece of Calcutta that definitely should not be missed because here the Raj doesn't just live, it simply never ended. The terribly English couple who still, thirty plus years after independence, run it, look like they've been time-warped."

The guidebook didn't tell the half of it. A bearer carried our luggage upstairs on his head; meals were announced with a gong; and tea and scones were served at midafternoon. Our host, Major Smith, a ramrod-straight British veteran of the Burma campaign, advised us: "Keep moving or she'll have you painted." It was true. A crew of painters was in constant motion, enamelling the decay of the Fairlawn in fluorescent green and peach, ordered about by Mrs. Lillian Smith (of Armenian descent) in fluent Bengali, Hindi, and English.

FOURTEEN FOLLOWED

AFTER YOU, MARK TWAIN

Our room was jammed with a sofa, two easy chairs, a tasselled floor lamp, desk, and dressing table, in addition to hard but comfortable twin beds. The double doors were secured from the inside by a four-foot iron bar which slid into a wooden slot. A latticework raft kept our feet out of the water draining from bathtub and sink into a channel in the concrete floor. The electricity went out soon after check-in, a frequent Calcutta happening. (Take flashlights.) But the room was clean, and good meals (both British and Indian) were served by turbanned waiters wearing white gloves. Morning tea was brought to our room. As far as we were concerned, the Fairlawn completely outstripped the Oriental. Fare at the Fairlawn was twenty-six dollars a day, all meals included. Besides, it was a lot more fun.

Best of all were the guests: an American ex-patriot living in Paris, a collector of antique Kashmiri shawls; a handsome Russian couple, fluent in English and ardent apologists for Soviet policy (she wore well-fitting designer jeans when they went out one night to the American movie, *The Blue Dolphin*); a Swedish doctor and his daughter, a nurse, working with Indian orphans; two British airline employees giving their vacation time and their airline passes to transport Indian babies for adoption in New York; a British film crew; a UNESCO couple searching for an apartment; a Catholic priest, confessor for the Sisters of Charity at nearby Mother Theresa's; a Canadian couple paying a nostalgic visit to Calcutta, their home for twenty years. The Canadians were our guides to the city, past and present, introducing us to the once posh department stores, import-export houses, private clubs, and office buildings, now filthy and deteriorating, on Chowringhee Road. Once a proud thoroughfare, it was now almost impassable, clogged by stalled traffic and yawning excavations for a mythical subway system already a decade in the making.

To see India is to see people in an astonishing diversity of appearance, color, costume, and speech. The splendor and squalor of their lives and the sheer numbers of them can best be experienced in Calcutta. It is said that anyone who has not seen Calcutta has not seen India, for here one finds less to inspect but more to see than in any other Indian city. In Calcutta the *sari* and the *dhoti* (loincloth) are still worn. Here the man-pulled rickshaw survives.

But Calcutta was a mistake from the start. It was chosen as a trading center by a British merchant named Job Charnock in 1690. It is up the twisting Hooghly River almost a hundred miles from the sea, on a steamy delta where disease is rife. Records from 1750 to 1850 indicate that of every one hundred British people arriving in any year, half would be dead in five years. Fevers and fluxes of every kind abounded—cholera, plague, smallpox, enteritis, dysentery, malaria—all with no cure. Remedies were cupping, bleeding, purging, and blistering, with an occasional resort to calomel, ipecac, or opium.

Death was so commonplace that there was almost no mourning. Emily Eden, an East India Company wife, wrote home to England in 1837: "You cannot imagine how the ranks close the very next day after death. ... Among the Europeans there are scarcely any old persons. ... It is melancholy to think how almost all of the people we have known at all intimately have in two years died off." Rudyard Kipling underscored the point:

> Ay, lay him 'neath the Simla pine—
> A fortnight fully to be missed.
> Behold, we lose our fourth at whist.
> A chair is vacant where we dine.

At the end of every monsoon the surviving Europeans

gathered for a banquet to celebrate the mere fact of survival.

Rudyard Kipling, who abhorred and loved Calcutta, called it the "City of Dreadful Night." He felt free to discuss what the fastidious Mark Twain was too polite to mention, the "Big Calcutta Stink":

> The dense smoke hangs low, in the chill of the morning, over an ocean of roofs, and, as the city wakes, there goes up to the smoke a deep, full-throated boom of life and motion and humanity. For this reason does he who sees Calcutta for the first time hang joyously out of the ticca-ghari [carriage] and sniff the smoke, and turn his face toward the tumult, saying: "This is a city. There is life here"... but has any one thoroughly investigated The Big Calcutta Stink? Benares is fouler in point of concentrated, pent-up muck, and there are local stenches in Peshawar which are stronger, but for diffused, soul-sickening expansiveness, the reek of Calcutta beats both. Bombay cloaks her stenches with a veneer of assafoetida and tobacco; Calcutta is above pretence.

It's hard to make olfactory comparisons with the air of almost ninety years ago, but it seems to me that the stench must have intensified. The city had less than a million inhabitants in those days. Today they are estimated to number ten million, although it is difficult to count people who have no homes and whose only possessions are on their backs or carried in a handkerchief.

Calcutta's urban decay set in when the British, recognizing their mistake, moved the capital to Delhi in 1911. After the Japanese attacked Pearl Harbor in 1941 and later moved into Burma, the British and Indian armies, together with thousands of Indians who worked in Burma, swarmed into Calcutta. Floods, famines, and communal rioting between Hindus and Muslims after partition of India in 1947 added more thousands as Hindu refugees arrived from East Pakistan.

Partition also robbed Calcutta of much of its economic base: the jute, rice, and tea of East Pakistan. Silting up of the harbor, deterioration of port facilities, and the erosion of capital—compounded by a communist-oriented political takeover of its government—all contributed to the decline. A tidal wave in the Bay of Bengal, epidemics, and the 1971 invasion by West Pakistan heaped disaster on disaster. All sent additional waves of refugees to Calcutta. India has now erected a barbed-wire fence along the Bangladesh border, a gesture laughable in its futility.

The Calcutta *Statesman* of February 7, 1896, reviewed Mark Twain's lecture of the previous evening under the headline HUMORIST ON THE HOOGHLY: "The quiet man who faces his audience most of the time with half-shut eyes and who speaks in a low monotone that gives one the idea that he is not thoroughly awake, somehow soon shows that he possesses the trick of bringing his thoughts before one with dramatic force. ... The humor lies not so much in the things said as in his manner of saying it. He sees that the essence of humor is the need for surprise, and when one least expects a joke, he fires it and is off again on some other tack."

Running down evidence of Mark Twain's visit to Calcutta consumed most of a day. We first stated the purpose of our visit to a guard at the office of the English-language newspaper, the *Statesman*, who led us to an official-looking man at a desk. Nonplussed by our request, the clerk summoned someone to guide us to the upstairs office of the secretary to the editor. This beautiful, sari-clad young woman immediately understood our mission and handed us a book of excerpts from the files of the *Statesman*, one of which was an account of Twain's visit.

This was interesting, but we wished to see the files. She said she'd explore the possibility, but in the meantime the editor would like to speak with us. The charming, elderly editor reminded me of my father and we hit it off immediately. He was delighted with the adventure of our journey and pleased to learn that somebody besides himself was aware that Mark Twain had visited Calcutta. Could he send a reporter to interview us?

Over tea, we discussed the business of newspapering in our two countries. There is no such thing as a weekly newspaper published in the villages of India. "What," the editor wanted to know, "would be the purpose of such publications?" I hadn't thought about this. The only justifications I could put forth arose from my background in a nation of literacy and self-government.

"Ah-chah!" said the editor in the all-encompassing Indian term of understanding and agreement.

In-house communication has not reached India. The editor summoned a guide to lead us to the top floor of the big, dingy building, where we explained to a wizened, old keeper of the newspaper's "morgue" our desire to see the 1896 files. He nodded, "Ah-chah," vanished, and emerged in minutes, smiling, and followed by an assistant carrying the needed file.

We marveled, knowing all too well the possibilities for loss or destruction during the decades since the British Raj, to say nothing of the ravages of that monsoon climate. When we expressed our surprise at the excellent condition of the newspapers, the proud librarian reminded us that newsprint in those days had been made with high rag content and no acid.

There being no such thing as a copying machine in the *Statesman*'s building, Winston and I spent the afternoon reading through the files and copying out accounts of

BRITISH POMP AND INDIAN COLOR

Mark Twain's visit. Countless cups of tea arrived while we paged through those ancient journals full of fascinating reportage of British rule over a supine subcontinent. At first we exchanged marvelous bits of information which kept diverting us from our task. Finally, we were forced to steel ourselves, bypass this treasure trove of history, and simply copy out the passages we sought, such as this editorial of February 8, 1896: "Mark Twain makes no secret of the cause of his vagabondage—the failure of the New York publishing firm in which his wife's fortune and his own hard-earned savings were embarked, spelt ruin. But we are glad to assure him that Englishmen in India, no less than English in every other part of the globe, know how to admire the manly independence and courage which bade him begin life anew with undaunted cheerfulness when over his head 60 summers have come and gone."

Mark Twain was a huge success in Calcutta, but what he really wanted to see was the Black Hole. He wrote in *Following the Equator:* "When a citizen finds himself in the capital of India he goes first of all to see the Black Hole of Calcutta—and is disappointed. The Black Hole was not preserved; it is gone long, long ago. It is strange. Just as it stood, it was itself a monument; a ready-made one. It was finished, it was complete, its materials were strong and lasting; it needed no furbishing up, no repairs; it merely needed to be let alone. ... And yet within the time of men who still live, the Black Hole was torn down and thrown away. ... There is no accounting for human beings."

Today's tourist is more likely to make a pilgrimage to see the work of Mother Theresa and her Sisters of Charity, not far from the Fairlawn Hotel. Outside stood a rabble of the poor and hungry, receiving portions of cooked rice ladled into proffered bowls and pans by a young woman under the wary eye of an elderly nun who seemed to know each applicant.

AFTER YOU, MARK TWAIN

The entrance to the training school was up a nearby alley. The orderliness of the clean-swept courtyard and the flowers surrounding the statue of the Blessed Virgin opposite the entrance were like an oasis in the Calcutta clamor. The sister who met us was apologetic that Mother Theresa was unavailable (we had not asked to see her), but she led us upstairs to where a priest was conducting mass for about thirty young Indian women, all in the order's white saris bordered in blue. The responses of the young voices, the hymns, and the obvious reverence all seemed fresh and lovely after the bedlam outside.

Sister Jonvan showed us a dormitory of the orphanage. The room, perhaps a hundred feet long, was filled with cribs and crawling with children. Toddlers tested their legs and played in the aisles and underneath the cribs, and held up their arms to be picked up. In a room off the dormitory, a dozen sisters held babies in their laps or gathered around them, while several hired women tended to the diapering in assembly-line fashion. A sister spooned food into the mouth of a tearful, big-eyed child, newly arrived, frightened and very hungry.

Outside on a balcony overlooking an open verandah, we watched a sister surrounded by twenty toddlers on potties—mass toilet training. A competition was in progress. It seemed to work. Around a corner, behind glass, were the abandoned newborns, many premature. The urgent bustle in the room continues night and day. On the floor under the viewing window was a tiny coffin, topped with a cross. In a hall a dozen retarded children were being cuddled and played with by four young women from DePauw University, doing their winter term here.

We noticed a cluster of nurses admiring a healthy looking toddler. "Why?" we asked Sister Jonvan. "Oh," she said, matter-of-factly. "He's a boy." She insisted on giving us a receipt for our gift. While we waited in an

anteroom, we noticed a sign: "Friends, please wait outside. We are sorry. There are no boys for adoption." An
Indian couple, looking very dejected, descended a stair-
way and handed Sister Jonvan a packet containing a gold
chain. She shook her head. "Sorry."

We did not have the courage to visit Mother Theresa's
home for the dying.

You can't see Calcutta from a hotel or a bus window.
You've got to get out where the people are. You must find
Jarmain Singh, our Sikh taxi driver, or reasonable fac-
simile. Almost all taxi drivers are Sikhs and almost all
Sikhs are called *Singh* (lion); it fits them. Red-turbanned
and fiercely bearded, Jarmain Singh attacked the
jampacked streets with horn blaring. He shouted greetings
to friends and epithets at pedestrians, rickshaw wallahs,
handcart pullers, truck drivers, and anyone else who
slowed our way. He stopped willingly, however, in mid-
traffic, for us to photograph a wedding procession and a
handsomely uniformed band, and buy a bouquet of red
roses from a hawker (twenty rupees, equivalent to twenty
cents)—oblivious to the horns of other drivers or the
resulting gridlock. He took us to the Howrah railroad
station, across the Hooghly River bridge, to the marble
palace of a maharajah, and to St. John's Anglican
churchyard where we discovered not the Black Hole of
Calcutta, but a monument to the 123 who died there. The
monument was commissioned by one of the 23 survivors of
the 146 incarcerated. Since independence it has been
moved here from the original site.

After our baptism by fire with Jarmain Singh, we
braved the city streets on foot, past beggars and families
of people living on the sidewalk outside our hotel. They
ate from a garbage dump adjoining a museum that houses
India's greatest collection of art and artifacts, as well as

AFTER YOU, MARK TWAIN

A RAILROAD STATION

100

a stuffed man- and woman-eating crocodile; from its stomach ornaments weighing fifteen pounds, fourteen ounces had been removed and are there displayed. We met a red-robed holy man, and five Hindu priests walking in single file behind a drummer, their noses and foreheads marked with white streaks like Iroquois warriors.

Calcutta is a wonder. In spite of its squalor, its people seem cheerful and purposeful. Even if their business consists of pawing through a garbage dump, they go to it with a will and a certain dignity. Their attitude is one of acceptance, probably a legacy of the caste system.

The Calcutta Metropolitan Development Authority exhibit at Victoria Memorial Hall, titled "Calcutta—Past, Present and Future," sketches the problems of the city and its forlorn hopes. Demands for water, transport, garbage and sewage disposal, health, education—all municipal services—are immense. But a plan has been devised and a start has been made on improved water supply and sanitation. A subway system has been attempted, and some additional housing (called with refreshing frankness "better bustees") has been built. An attempt is also being made to interest and involve citizens in plans for the future. Given the economic prospects for the city and, for that matter, all of Bengal, and the negative impact of its government, the odds against improvement are overwhelming.

A major problem may be the Bengalis themselves. Organization is not their talent and they seem to resent authority. Among the most irreverent of them was the poet, Sir Rabindranath Tagore, who won the Nobel prize for literature in 1913, and who composed the words for both the Indian and Bangladesh national anthems. He was born in Calcutta and lived there most of his life. It's too bad Mark Twain didn't meet him; they had a lot in common. Consider these random reflections from Tagore's book of poems, *Fireflies:*

AFTER YOU, MARK TWAIN

The sectarian thinks
that he has the sea
ladled into his private pond.

To justify their own spilling of ink
they spell the day as night.

The worm thinks it strange and foolish
that man does not eat his books.

The same sun is newly born in new lands
in a ring of endless dawns.

New Delhi airport seemed immaculate after Calcutta.
The night streets of the city were wide, empty, and clean.
It was 10 P.M. when we arrived at Claridge's Hotel. We
followed a glittering bridegroom on a white horse, preceded
by a band marching up the driveway to a green-and-white
striped marquee bright with colored lights and festooned
with flowers. Carpets covered the lawn. Bearded,
turbanned men milled about. Before we could make our
way to the elevator, the bride in her red sari came slowly
down the marble staircase. She shimmered with jewels.
She was lovely. Bejewelled mothers, aunts, sisters,
cousins, and friends followed. It was a stunning reception.
    We slept late on Sunday morning and read the *Times
of India*. There were two pages of "matrimonials."
Samples: "Wanted a suitable match for Punjabi girl, 160
cms. [five feet, one inch tall], beautiful, smart, and doing
her MS in gynaecology & obstetrics. The match must be
from a respectable small family, minimum 172 cms., fair
with good features sober habits and no spects. [spec-
tacles?] Preferably MD/MS doctor in teaching profession
or well-established engineer of multi-national company
or in administrative job. Those who do not meet these

requirements need not write, others may write straight with photo." "Homely and beautiful bride for Arora boy 23/176 cms. B.Comm., slim, handsome, smart, does business in West U.P. [Uttar Pradesh, an Indian state], owns property of considerable value, handsome income."

It was the wedding season. The hotel manager assured us we were welcome to observe and photograph, but wait, he said, "This is nothing." He was right. The hotel afforded constant entertainment. Subsequent bridegrooms arrived on elephants and camels, but all were eclipsed by one who must have been a maharajah in a flower-covered carriage drawn by six white horses. He and his entourage paraded down the road to meet his bride at another hotel, lighted through the darkness by dozens of people carrying Coleman lanterns on their heads. This Arabian Nights display of wealth was a shock after the poverty of Calcutta.

The British, during their years in India—first as the British East India Company and then as the British Raj—left their mark. It is visible everywhere in New Delhi, but nowhere as apparent as in the combined British pomp and Indian color of the annual Republic Day Parade on January 26. As we were finding our seats, a helicopter costumed as a richly caparisoned elephant waddled through the sky over the bleachers, showering tinsel over the crowd.

Prime Minister Indira Ghandi, wearing a gold sari and standing in an open jeep (making an excellent target) waved to the crowd as she was driven the length of the parade route to the reviewing stand. "Gutsy lady," Winston remarked, as we joined in the cheers. (I reminded him of his remark six months later when she was assassinated by her Sikh bodyguards.) The president arrived in his ceremonial carriage, preceded by his mounted bodyguard. A twenty-one-gun salute and the national anthem launched the show.

AFTER YOU, MARK TWAIN

For two hours mounted cavalry carried out precise drills, and marching columns of men with brilliant uniforms and stiffly starched headdresses called *puggrees* marched past. Pipe majors swaggered in Campbell tartan or Royal Stuart, tossing their maces before kilted bagpipers. Camels and elephants, costumed more beautifully than circus animals, shambled by in platoons. Tableaus from the states, boys and girls of the National Cadet corps imitating their elders, folk dancers from the provinces, and a flypast by the Indian air force wound up the show. It was a spectacular day's entertainment.

The next evening, almost its equal was performed—the Beating of Retreat, a ceremonial display of performing bands, commemorating the days when war was civilized and armies retired from the field at sunset to rest for the next day's battle. It ended with the camel corps outlined like statues against the sunset on the capital parapets, while massed bands played "Abide With Me"— a strangely British and Christian benediction in this Hindu land. Then came fireworks! India is full of surprises.

There's plenty to see and do in Delhi. Nobody should leave the country without experiencing classical Indian dance or seeing the sound and light show at the Red Fort, where conquering armies seem to sweep over the land once again.

Heera Kapasi, U.S. Information Service librarian, directed us to the India International Centre and arranged for a meeting with H. K. Kaul, librarian, author, and editor of *Travellers' India, An Anthology*. Consisting of extracts from more than four hundred accounts by visitors, from antiquity to the twentieth century, it includes several Mark Twain excerpts. (Books are a bargain in India, and bookstores easily found.) Mr. Kaul was kind enough to spend an hour with me, over tea, sharing his enthusiasm for Mark Twain, making suggestions for research, and recommending that I attend a lecture at the center that evening by Sir Cyril Henry Phillips, an eminent authority on Indian history. The subject was "The Rationale of the British East India Company, 1750–1850."

Sir Cyril looked and sounded like a product of central casting. The audience was made up almost entirely of distinguished looking older Indians, who might well have stepped out of the movie *Ghandhi*. If they themselves hadn't been involved in the independence movement, surely their fathers had.

Sir Cyril had made a study of the British East India Company, established in 1600 by the royal assent of Elizabeth, by the Grace of God Queen of England, and lasting until the Great Mutiny of 1857. The lecturer opened his remarks by saying that there had been an enormous difference between the policy and practice of the British East India Company. Economics dictated the need for expansion of the empire. Study of the company's records over the years showed, however, that trade was in India's favor and, according to the speaker, the company's purpose was government, not trade.

Its entering wedge was to introduce European education to India in an effort to raise the economic and social level of the people. For this purpose the company introduced European school teachers into India—"one of the greatest benefits that it was to confer on the country," said Sir Cyril. He quoted John Stuart Mill, who said the British East India Company was the "most enlightened government in the world at that time."

Sir Cyril had barely concluded his remarks and thrown the meeting open to questions when a gentleman who had been growling to himself during the lecture rose and challenged the whole premise of the evening. His argument: Sir Cyril and the British East India Company operated on the mistaken assumption that when the British arrived on the subcontinent, there was no political system, no organized government, no education in place. Actually, he said, India had flowered under the rule of the Moghul emperors as it never has since. The Emperor Akbar had united India and established a stable government which fixed a fair rent for the peasant, steady revenue for the treasury, rule by impartial officers who were responsible to him, and, furthermore, Muslims peacefully lived with Hindus. As for education, Indians had been more literate than Europeans of that time and more literate than they ever were under the British. The British had hardly done India a favor by establishing a system of education to serve the company's needs. The gentleman took his seat to enthusiastic applause from the audience. It was obvious that debate would go on far into the night.

There was not a taxi, scooter, or rickshaw in sight. Realizing that I could not safely hazard the long walk to the hotel through Lodi Gardens, I explained my predicament to an Indian gentleman unlocking his car. "Of course," he replied, "I drive right past the Claridge."

Discussing the lecture en route, this former Indian ambassador to Japan and I agreed that imperialism simply doesn't work. I thought the ambassador's remarks eminently logical: "Imperialism is against human nature," he said. "People living together want to be liked. This is not possible when one country is subjugated by another." The ambassador went on to describe what he had observed in Japan after World War II. Because the United States had treated the Japanese fairly and intelligently, today the two countries are allies, and business partners.

Although dinner guests were awaiting his return home, it now being the traditional late hour for Indian dining, we talked at the hotel entrance for some time while I explained our Mark Twain journey and he told of the struggle for independence.

Two million graves of Scots, Irish, and English people are scattered throughout India, and there's no way of calculating the loneliness, hardships, separations, and effort spent. After almost 350 years, the British handed India back. Mark Twain's thoughtful insights on India, past, present, and future, are relevant today:

> India had the start of the whole world in the beginning of things. ... She had wealth; she was populous with deep thinkers and subtle intellects; she had mines and woods and fruitful soil. It would seem as if she should have kept the lead, and should be today not the meek dependent of an alien master, but mistress of the world, and deliver law and command to every tribe and nation in it. But, in truth, there was never any possibility of such supremacy for her. If there had been but one India and one language—but there were 80 of them! Where there are 80 nations and several hundred governments, fighting and quarreling must be the common business of life; unity of purpose and policy are impossible.

When a travel agent tells you that with a round-the-world airline ticket, you can visit any ongoing stop en route, get it in writing. Mark Twain went to Agra and saw the Taj Mahal, "the most celebrated construction on the earth." He compared it to a New England ice storm. Not nearly as famous as the Taj Mahal, but equally marvelous, are the caves of Ellora and Ajanta near the city of Aurangabad. We wanted to go there. Indian Airlines maintained that, although the flight from New Delhi to Bombay landed at Aurangabad, it would not be possible for us to stop there. We must fly on to Bombay, then pay for a round-trip flight back to Aurangabad—more than three hundred dollars extra. After a lengthy argument and subsequent appeals to resident higher-ups, the office director scribbled "special case" on our ticket and let us stop at Aurangabad for thirty-six dollars.

Travelling Americans with similar interests become instant friends in India. We had encountered Mary Ann and Gene Schum from Hamilton, Ohio, at a lecture and then at a dance recital in New Delhi, and had dined with them at our hotel. We were pleased when they boarded our plane at Udaipur, where they had stayed the night in a beautiful palace-turned-hotel. We shared a taxi with them from the airport at Aurangabad to the Ashoka Hotel, and later for the drive to the Ellora Caves.

Hewn from the stone of a sloping sidehill into temples and monastaries and *stupas* (tower-shaped shrines) by Buddhists, Hindus, and Jains from the fourth to twelfth centuries, the caves predate the temples of Angkor Wat in Cambodia. There are thirty-four separate shrines. The religious fervor possessing these people is incomprehensible to a twentieth-century American. Generations of monks and priests and students lived and worshipped here before the images of the Buddha and the Hindu gods, while succeeding generations of architects and masons and sculptors labored to make each structure more impressive than the last.

The calm contemplation of the Buddhist caves, depicting the life of Buddha, contrasts with the energy, flamboyance, and overwhelming size of the Hindu caves. One of these is three stories high (or deep depending on your viewpoint), ornamented with elephants, serpents, crocodiles, bulls, and all manner of livestock, in addition to an unending procession of Hindu deities in all their manifestations. "India has two million gods, and worships them all. In religion all other countries are paupers; India is the only millionaire," wrote Mark Twain. Unfortunately, at five o'clock the guards shooed us out. There was not enough time.

We left the hotel at seven the next morning for the

BRITISH POMP AND INDIAN COLOR

Ajanta Caves—a drive of an hour and a half past mud-walled huts, poor farms, and processions of peasants carrying brass water jugs, bundles of reeds, and baskets of all sizes. The road was clogged with bicycles, bullock carts, a few buses, and trucks, all on the move. Wherever one looked life proceeded toward the securing of the day's food. Farmers were in their fields. A woman winnowed grain. Children were everywhere, and animals—a grossly pregnant pig, goats, dogs, cows.

At the Ajanta Caves a rabble of entrepreneurs exploded with wares from rock crystals to sweets to offers to guide or, better still, to carry us up the steep climb in four-man open *palanquins*. "Two miles, two miles!" they shouted. It wasn't two miles, but it was hot and it was a tough climb. Mary Ann Schum took them up. I did not envy her. The ride was precarious up the steep and uneven stone steps to the caves. Besides, I would be embarrassed to have four of these skinny, albeit wiry, men carry my big, strong American frame up such an incline.

The Ellora Caves were never lost, but the Ajanta Caves, which are famous for paintings rather than their carvings, were abandoned during the decline of Buddhism in India, and were rediscovered in 1819 by a British hunting party. Carved some two thousand years ago into the rimrock, from the top down and without scaffolding, their physical and spiritual impact is stunning.

Each seems to be a separate cloister with dormitories, dining and meeting halls, fronted by an elegant verandah overlooking the valley below. Images of the Buddha in his various incarnations stand in niches, and sumptuous scenes from his life and temptation cover the walls. Even the ceilings are painted to look like Persian carpets. Art historians believe that these murals were painted by successive families of artists who trained each new generation in their artistic tradition.

Our eyes grew tired in the uncertain sunlight, deflected into the interiors (for a price) by attendants holding mirrors. We had brought flashlights, but trying to view the wide expanses of these intricate murals by that weak and intermittent glow was futile. We left at the end of the day exhausted. Although time, vandalism, moisture, and defacement by devout Muslims (who regard depiction of the human face and figure as blasphemy) have left their marks, the astonishingly beautiful overall effect remains.

I envy Mark Twain his memories of Bombay: "Even now, after the lapse of a year, the delirium of those days in Bombay has not left me and I hope it never will." Today's Bombay is not as he remembered it. Before we landed, the captain announced that there was a general strike and that transportation from the airport into the city was not available. Braced by our experience in Calcutta, we wondered what uniquely Indian solution would present itself.

It didn't take long. A young man sitting beside Winston offered to take charge of us, explaining that it was an attempt to repay the many kindnesses he and his wife had received while studying in the United States. The scene at the airport duplicated that in Calcutta—confusion, not a taxi, not a bus, not a rickshaw. A few private cars left laden with Indians and their baggage. Instructing us to wait in front of the terminal, our friend disappeared through the crowd, returning in ten minutes to seize our suitcases and shout, "Follow me." We did, gratefully, to a lone, rickety local bus, parked out of sight of the terminal entrance. It took us within a block of our hotel. Our friend carried my bag to the lobby, wished us well and bade us a smiling goodbye.

During our fourteen-mile journey from the airport

into India's commercial center, past mile after mile of squalid bustees, our rescuer described the trauma of his return to Bombay. Almost anyone can find a job of some kind here, he told us, as a kind of apology for the hovels. What they can't find is a place to live.

"When my wife and I left to study in the United States, we made a vow that we would return to Bombay to work. We are both engineers. We were not going to be part of the brain drain, but when we returned we had culture shock. The poverty was here when we left, but it seemed to have gotten worse. What really shocked us was the acceptance of it. People say things are getting better, but it seems to us that the poor are just as poor as ever and there are more of them. ... Well, here we are. And here we will stay."

As we neared the city, office towers and highrise apartments gleamed in the evening light, and hordes of pedestrians, grounded by the transportation strike, made their way to their hovels or highrises in a silent, unmotorized rush hour. It was a scene Mark Twain might have viewed from a horse-drawn carriage en route from the wharf to the hotel: "Tramp, tramp, tramping along the road, in singles, couples, groups and gangs, you have the workingman and the workingwoman."

But Bombay's working people are no longer costumed to be road decorations, the men "nobly-built athletes with not a rag on but a loin-handkerchief," nor are the women "slender, shapely creatures, as erect as lightning rods with only a bright-colored piece of stuff wound about head and body," and carrying "shiny brass water jars of graceful shape" on their heads.

Twain particularly noticed the color of their skin: "Nearly all black and brown skins are beautiful, but a beautiful white skin is rare. ... Where dark complexions are massed, they make the whites look bleached out,

A lady. Complexion, new parchment.
Another lady. Complexion, old parchment.
Another. Pink and white, very fine.
Man. Grayish skin, with purple areas.
Man. Unwholesome fish-belly skin.
Girl. Sallow face, sprinkled with freckles.
Old woman. Face whitey-gray.
Young butcher. Face a general red flush.
Jaundiced man — mustard yellow.
Elderly lady. Colorless skin, with two conspicuous moles.
Elderly man — a drinker. Boiled-cauliflower nose in a flabby face veined with purple crinklings.
Healthy young gentleman. Fine fresh complexion.
Sick young man. His face a ghastly white.

unwholesome and sometimes frankly ghastly. ... As for the Indian brown—firm, smooth, blemishless, pleasant and restful to the eye, afraid of no color, harmonizing with all colors and adding grace to them all—I think there is no sort of chance for the average white complexion against that rich and perfect tint."

He would have been disappointed in the bank tellers and secretaries and store clerks of commercial Bombay today. Trousers and skirts have displaced the cool and practical *saris*, *dhotis*, and *luingis* (wraparound skirts worn by men), especially among the young on Bombay's streets. The crowds walking along the road that evening were notably uncolorful, intent only on reaching their homes and their evening curries.

BOMBAY BRACES UP FOR BANDH, was the headline in the *Times* of India: "All public transport, including buses, taxis and rickshaws are off the roads and Opposition leaders have warned the people that it could be dangerous to travel by the suburban trains." It was expected to be one of the biggest *bandhs* (general strikes) in recent history, supported by trade unions and parties opposed to Indira Gandhi's party, and backing the farmers who were demanding compensation for their land which had been requisitioned for port facilities. Two prominent labor union leaders who, according to the newspaper, "had been at daggers drawn for some time, had joined hands to make the bandh a success."

"Hang loose" must be the traveller's motto. It was lucky that our hotel was centrally located. We could at least walk the streets of the downtown district and explore the famous Taj Mahal Hotel. Its lobby was swarming with backpackers, tourists, an assortment of Arab sheiks, and guests who had come to the city to attend a wedding uniting two prominent Bombay families; all were stranded. We window-shopped the posh stores of the hotel and watched the crowd until we were hungry.

An American businessman sitting at a nearby table at the hotel's Shamiana restaurant apologized for the disarray. A patron of twenty years, he had never seen such a commotion. The Taj Mahal is really two hotels—an elegant, colonial structure built around a balconied court, and the multistoried Taj International, an expensive and undistinguished Howard Johnson-style addition. The lonely American invited us to view his suite in the colonial wing. It was spectacularly beautiful, and confirmed our Bangkok opinion that such hotels are for those on an expense account.

It also established that Bombay demonstrates the ultimate in extremes of poverty and wealth. It is a far cry from Calcutta. Although with eight and a half million people it is almost as large, and attracts almost five hundred new residents a day, the newcomers arrive as job seekers, not refugees. And they have hope. They come here by choice, harboring the dream that life will be better here than in the village they came from. At least it is more exciting. With luck they hope for upward mobility, if only from pavement dwelling to the slums, where at least half of the population live. In some ways Bombay and India have changed little in the ninety years since Mark Twain wrote:

> This is indeed India; the land of dreams and romance, of fabulous wealth and fabulous poverty, of splendor and rags, of palaces and hovels, of famine and pestilence, of genii and giants and Aladdin lamps, of tigers and elephants, the cobra and the jungle, the country of a hundred nations and a hundred tongues, of a thousand religions and two million gods, cradle of the human race, birthplace of human speech, mother of history, grandmother of legend, great-grandmother of tradition ... the one land that all men desire to see, and having seen once, by even a

glimpse, would not give that glimpse for the shows of all the rest of the globe combined.

India, starting with Bombay, was Mark Twain's favorite country on his equatorial journey. The love affair was mutual. The *Bombay Gazette* of January 25, 1896, noted: "The large number of Parsis present—to say nothing of a good sprinkling of Mahomedans and Hindus—was a noteworthy evidence of the cosmopolitan character of Mark Twain's popularity."

When the British acquired the seven islands that make up Bombay, it was a fishing village. The Parsis' talent for business made Bombay so prosperous that today landfill has joined the seven islands into one city, which is even now dispersing into suburbs. Although there are only about eighty thousand Parsis, they control a disproportionate share of industry and wealth, and they have evinced a considerable sense of civic responsibility. They have endowed numerous cultural, medical, and educational institutions. This is one explanation of the difference between Calcutta and Bombay.

Determined to see something of Mark Twain's Bombay in spite of the bandh, we took the single bus tour available in the city. We were the only non-Indians on the bus, which stopped at the Gateway of India, the Prince of Wales Museum, the Hanging Gardens, the Nehru Science Centre, the aquarium, Malabar Point, the Parsi Towers of Silence on Malabar Hill, and the Mahatma Gandhi Museum. There the room where Gandhi lived, studied, and spun is kept as he left it. Unhurried, unpressured, with a well-informed and well-spoken Indian woman guide, the tour was a good introduction to Bombay. The Indians seemed pleased and surprised that Americans would be taking such a tour with them.

Getting to the airport presented a problem. The

bandh still held. Nothing moved. To catch the morning flight to Sri Lanka, we set out at dawn. Baksheesh produced a decrepit cab and a nervous driver. He scanned the street warily before leaving the parking lot. Only rickshaws, bicycles, bullock carts and pedestrians were moving. But he proved himself fearless on the road to the airport. We tore past the unspeakable cardboard slums and made it to the terminal before full light. It was a relief to be getting out of India without having been maimed in a traffic accident or having killed any pedestrians.

A handful of harried passengers waited in the departure lounge. A tall young woman, obviously American, was wearing conspicuously played-in tennis shoes. She explained that her shoes had been stolen from the entrance of the Ghandi memorial in New Delhi. Conventional walking shoes for large American feet are unavailable in India.

A pale-faced American businessman confided, "I've been sick again. I get sick every time I come to India and I come here twice a year. ... It's my own fault. I don't like drinks without ice, so it happens every time. The trouble is that I meet with businessmen and officials over cocktails. Actually, I like this part of the world so much that it's worth it."

Leaving India we flew over village country, mudflats, seacoast, and then to the top of the teardrop that is Sri Lanka, dropped by Krishna, according to Hindu legend, off India's tip. Washed by the waters of the Bay of Bengal on the east and the Arabian Sea on the west, at one point it is only thirty-one miles from India.

CHAPTER VII

Resplendent Land: Sri Lanka

> I was in Cairo years ago. That was Oriental,
> but there was a lack. When you are in Florida or
> New Orleans you are in the South—that is granted;
> but you are not in the South. ... Ceylon was Oriental
> in the last measure of completeness—utterly Oriental,
> also utterly tropical. ... All the requisites were
> present ... that smother of heat, heavy with odors of
> unknown flowers, and that sudden invasion of purple
> bloom fissured with lightnings—then the tumult of
> crashing thunder and the downpour ... nothing was
> lacking. And away off in the deeps of the jungle and
> in the remoteness of the mountains were the ruined
> cities and mouldering temples, mysterious relics of
> the pomps of a forgotten time and a vanished race.
>
> Mark Twain

Ceylon was originally a paradise to be sacked. Every thing was there. And everything conceivable was collected and shipped to Europe: precious stones—sapphires, rubies, star sapphires, alexandrites, pearls, tourmalines, cat's eyes, coral; seven kinds of cinnamon, cardamom, pepper, ginger, mustard oil, citronella; calamander, palmyra root, tamarind, sandalwood; wild indigo, deer horns, elephant tusks, hog lard, rubber, coconuts, tea, rice, cocoa, tobacco. The Portuguese, the Dutch, and the British took turns at hauling off the loot. King Solomon had been there before them, picking up jewels for the Queen of Sheba. So had Sinbad the Sailor and Marco Polo. But the British got the most. Ceylon was a British colony from 1796 to 1948.

In those days, sea captains approaching the island would sprinkle cinnamon on the decks and summon passengers to come and "smell Ceylon" while they were still ten miles out at sea. They called it the fragrant isle. After independence in 1948, the Sinhalese changed the name of their country to Sri Lanka, "Resplendent Land." But it was known to ancient mariners as the Island of Serendip. From it came the word *serendipity*—the gift of finding valuable or agreeable things not sought for. According to Muslim legend, it was a Garden of Eden.

Sri Lanka is so near the equator that it has no appreciable seasons and the length of daylight hardly varies. You can catch the spectacular sunsets every evening at seven year-round. Only 270 miles from north to south, and 140 miles at its greatest width, it is almost joined to the Indian mainland by a series of islands called Adam's Bridge. Across these islands the Hindu hero, Rama, is said to have walked to recover his wife, Sita, who had been abducted by the king of Lanka.

Located on a quiet street in Colombo's Cinnamon Gardens residential area, the Cinnamon Gardens Inn was quietly inviting. Houseparents of our daughter when she was at the American International School in New Delhi had told us of the inn. Single-storied wings surrounded a courtyard garden of tropical foliage, made cool by a miniature waterfall and goldfish pond. The lobby and hallways were furnished with antique chests, chairs, side-boards, and knick-knacks—the leavings of three and a half centuries of Portuguese, Dutch, and British colonial homemakers who couldn't take all their treasures with them when time ran out.

A smiling young Sinhalese woman in a short *choli* (vest) and wrapped sarong welcomed us. She proved to be our friend and adviser. After days of stuffy hotels with carpeted floors, it was refreshing to have clean, polished quarry tile. The window of our room opened onto the garden. The whole atmosphere was quiet and cool and serendipitous.

RESPLENDENT LAND: SRI LANKA

It was Ground Hog Day at home.

We arranged for a car and driver to take us into the interior to the "ruined cities and mouldering temples." When it arrived at the Cinnamon Gardens Inn early the next morning, it was a black limousine equipped to carry diplomatic flags. This ostentatious transport was somewhat of an embarrassment to us, but in the days to come we grew to appreciate its comfort, as well as its driver, Jaya Sundera. Highway maintenance has flagged since the British departed after nationalization of the tea and rubber estates in 1956. The washouts of the rainy season had further narrowed the road. Jaya was a good driver.

We drove in the morning steam north from Colombo along the western edge of the teardrop. We had envisioned sandy beaches and fishing villages on the shore of the Indian Ocean, but the highway was a tunnel through groves of coconut trees and intermittent jungle. We never glimpsed the ocean. It began to rain and the tropical downpour lasted all day. Our limousine plowed through torrents of blood-red runoff, meeting or passing few cars, buses, bullock carts, or pedestrians.

The sun came out as we drove into the grounds of Tissa Wewa Guest House at Anuradhapura. (Sinhalese names must be tackled slowly and carefully, syllable by syllable, with the accent on the next-to-last syllable. An-u-rad-ha-*pur*-a. Pol-o-nnar-u-*woo*-a.) At Tissa Wewa— shades of the departed British—chintz-cushioned rattan chairs and woven *charpoys* (string beds) furnished the wide verandahs enjoyed by guests and a company of mischievous monkeys. Tea was served on the verandah. Dinner was announced by a gong. Seating places were assigned in the dining room.

We'd been eating curry all through India and Bangladesh, but this was the first time I had a lesson on how to eat it properly. After I'd helped myself to a

substantial portion of rice, small dishes of curried vegetables, meat and shrimp were passed around. I placed a
spoonful of the first of these beside my rice. Quickly, a
small waiter was at my elbow shaking his head. "No,
madam." He scooped out a teacup-sized crater in the rice,
and dumped some of each curry into the hole. I thanked
him, and set to eating, only to be interrupted once more.
"No, madam." Taking my fork, he pushed in the sides of
the excavation and expertly mucked the curries with the
rice. Once again I thanked him. He was right. It was
delicious.

At our table, an Australian couple who had been
everywhere from Chile to Yugoslavia announced the dis-
tances they had travelled as a kind of scorecard. A woman
ate at a table by herself. I inquired as we left the dining
room whether she had been naughty and wasn't allowed to
eat with the grown-ups. "You must be an American," she
laughed. "Nobody else would notice." A student of Buddhism, she was here with Sinhalese friends and was living
in a separate cottage away from the guest house—hence
her exclusion. She had spent a bad night because there
was no electricity in her cottage and she had been
frightened. I didn't think until later that I should have
given her my flashlight.

We left after breakfast to visit the ruins of the sacred
city of Anuradhapura, the island's first capital. A planned
city with an extensive system of tanks and conduits to
store and transport water, and a regimented arrangement
for housing the various castes and occupations and religions, it had been the citadel of the Vijaya dynasty and
the setting for successive murderous invasions by the
princes and armies of southern India.

Buddhism was brought here by a priest in 246 B.C.,
and a branch from the sacred Bo tree under which Buddha had received his enlightenment was brought from

RESPLENDENT LAND: SRI LANKA

India and planted. It is this ancient tree, its age at the time of our visit authenticated at some twenty-two hundred years, which makes Anuradhapura a place of pilgrimage for Buddhists. The tree, a wild fig, has grown to immense size, and its spreading branches are buttressed on all sides by wooden props. It is surrounded by a gold fence and a circle of meditating Buddhists, both saffron-robed monks and ordinary pilgrims.

You can't visit Sri Lanka and the shrines of this ancient religion without wondering about its appeal. Buddhism is a philosophical system, tolerant of other religions, non-proselytizing, and advocating "the middle way." It teaches forgiveness of enemies and avoidance of injury to others. Through the extinction of desire and individual consciousness, Buddhists seek enlightenment and *nirvana*, the state of a perfect and tranquil mind. Motive is the measure of morality, rather than the total of good or bad actions of a life. The chief end of the disciple is to know and practice the teachings of Buddha and to achieve a state of mystic meditation.

That is the inspiration for the thousands of statues of Buddha throughout Sri Lanka, Burma, India, Thailand, Cambodia, China, and Japan. To westerners it appears that the devout are worshipping the images, but Buddhists say a likeness helps them in their meditation. Buddha did not claim to be a god. He was a teacher. Nevertheless, the proliferation of images, stupas, shrines, moon stones, pagodas, and *dagabas* (bell-shaped shrines holding relics of the Buddha), many with attendant monasteries, boggles the mind of the traveller. Devout kings and wealthy merchants sought to achieve excellence of character by donating land and treasure to the Buddhist priesthood, who erected ever more costly monuments over the centuries.

The ultimate Buddhas were in Polonnaruwooa. We reached their location, called Gal Vihara, in a steady rain and rented umbrellas from a small boy to walk a thousand yards down a muddy path. Located in an uncluttered area under trees, these colossal statues are carved out of living granite. They stand before a simple granite backdrop— seated, standing, and reclining sculptures, stunning in their size and simplicity. The reclining Buddha measures forty-six feet and the standing one twenty-three feet.

Opposite, on a flat outcropping, several men sat meditating under umbrellas in the rain. I would have liked to join them, but instead committed the sight to memory. Perhaps it was the dim light, or viewing them through the rain, but the impact of those statues makes me forget all the other hundreds of Buddhas we saw before and after. Thomas Merton, a Trappist monk who saw the Buddhas of Polonnaruwa in 1968 just a few days before he died, wrote:

> The great smiles. Huge and yet subtle. Filled with every possibility, questioning nothing, knowing everything, rejecting nothing. ... The thing about all this is that there is no puzzle, no problem, and really no "mystery." All problems are resolved and everything is clear, simply because what matters is clear. ... everything is emptiness and everything is compassion. ... This is Asia in its purity, not covered over with garbage, Asian or European or American, and it is clear, pure, complete. It says everything; it needs nothing. And because it needs nothing it can afford to be silent, unnoticed, undiscovered. It does not need to be discovered. It is we, Asians included, who need to discover it.

It was only a short drive to the royal citadel of Sigiriya. We were advised not to attempt to climb the rock fortress during the heat of the day, so we waited until late afternoon to tackle the fifteen-hundred-year-old Lion's Rock. It was built as a refuge by King Kasyapa, who had murdered his father. A narrow walkway chiseled into the side of a monolithic granite mountain passes a "mirror wall," smoothed beyond belief and painted with lifesized murals of voluptuous heavenly maidens casting down flowers upon mortal men. That these paintings have survived the ravages of the tropics for centuries is a miracle.

Before the final assault, we rested on the giant paws of the stone lions guarding the upward steps to the ruins of six acres of splendid palaces, apartments, and pleasure gardens which occupied the whole mountaintop. Eighteen years after Kasyapa built this fortress, challenged by the army of his half-brother, he killed himself with a dagger when he thought his supporters had abandoned him.

The quality of the stonework and the vistas over the surrounding jungle are reminiscent of Machu Picchu in Peru, although the absence of higher peaks and thin Andean air gives the Sri Lankan abandoned fortress an entirely different aura. The similarity of design between these two impregnable mountaintop cities, conceived by such dissimilar cultures on opposite sides of the globe, is arresting.

The caves of Dumbulla were of little interest to us after seeing those at Ellora and Ajanta, particularly since they are natural, not excavated by worshippers. The endless Buddhas they contained were by now only repititious, and nothing compared to the Polonnaruwa Buddhas. But at least the caves were cool after our scramble up over stone outcroppings in the heat of the afternoon. It was refreshing to visit a spice garden near the town of Matale where cinnamon, nutmeg, clove, mace, camphor, allspice, and pepper grow on trees. It all smelled simply grand.

Now we were headed south to the high mountain center of the island, passing schoolgirls in the starched white uniforms stipulated by the government. When Mark Twain visited, girls were not educated and therefore not uniformed, except in mission schools, an innovation about which he was disparaging: "Into this dream of fairyland and paradise a grating dissonance was injected. Out of a missionary school came marching, two and two, sixteen prim and pious little Christian black girls, Europeanly clothed—dressed to the last detail as they would have been dressed on a summer Sunday in an English or American village. Those clothes—oh, they were unspeakably ugly! Ugly, barbarous, destitute of taste, destitute of grace, repulsive as a shroud."

It was late afternoon when we dipped into the royal city of the Kandian kings. When the British conquered Kandy in 1815, they ended a monarchy that had ruled for more than twenty-three centuries. Built around an artificial mirror lake with a beautiful islet in the center, bordered by a low stone wall and walkway, it invites leisurely exploration. The Temple of the Sacred Tooth, one of the most photographed buildings in the world, casts its perfect reflection in the lake.

Every traveller describes the Temple of the Tooth— Buddha's sacred tooth, that is, which is not really *the* tooth because the Catholic Portuguese got possession of it and burned it upon instructions of their archbishop. But Sinhalese priests manufactured another tooth which has proven quite satisfactory. While the veneration of any tooth, let alone a fake tooth, strikes one as odd, pilgrims nevertheless visit the temple in a steady stream, each bringing cash offerings and fragrant white flowers which fill the building with perfume.

The entrance to the main temple is flanked by two pairs of pillar-like elephant tusks which guard the steps leading up to the sanctuary where the tooth is kept. Here, behind iron bars, in a gilded shrine shaped like a bell, the Sacred Tooth lies in the smallest of six nested caskets of decreasing size, all of solid gold and set with precious stones. The tooth is on display only on rare occasions to persons of high rank. We didn't see it. Nowhere in the east did we see so many monks and acolytes in saffron robes nor experience such an atmosphere of reverence and mysticism.

The ten-day Festival of the August Moon is held annually to honor the Sacred Tooth. It features the temple elephant, his tusks sheathed in gold, walking on a silk carpet and carrying the jeweled relic casket within a golden howdah. Nearly a hundred elephants and a thousand drummers and dancers take part in the pageant, in which the famous Kandy Dance Ensemble stars.

We saw this troop perform in an evening's entertainment which outdid anything we had seen in the way of gymnastics—folk dances, religious dances, exorcising dances with devil masks, plate twirlers, acrobats doing terrifying backflips, dances with fire and with sticks. During the show a barbecue pit was smoldering to one side of the stage, and as the performance ended the coals were glowing red hot. It was not for steaks but for a fire walker. We had not bargained for this. I sat next to a Dutch pathologist who said he had seen fire walking many times, and assured me it is no fake.

Sri Lanka is infinite variety. The Kandy newspaper reported that the majority of the city's telephones were out of order. Even the commander of the army and the mayor were without phone service. "What purpose do these telephones serve?" the newspaper asked. The same paper carried this poem:

AFTER YOU, MARK TWAIN

THE HEN

A woman came to the
         door today
to sell
Her hen.

Around her wrist
She wore a pirith thread.
She didn't ask for alms.

She only wanted
to sell
Her hen.

She told me her little
         daughter cried
Because she (the daughter)
         knew her plans
to sell
The hen.

And now
The boy has brought
         onto my table
Snug in my curry pan
The milkwhite hen.

And still the little girl
Mixes with her tears
The rice
Her mother bought
With the money
I gave her for
The hen.

                H. Chula Piyadasa

RESPLENDENT LAND: SRI LANKA

If it's true that the Garden of Eden was in Sri Lanka, it was surely located at Peradeniya just four miles from Kandy. Once the pleasure gardens of a Kandian queen, the Royal Botanical Gardens show what nature can accomplish when given optimum conditions and optimum care. Gorgeously landscaped, they seemingly exhibit every plant and tree that can be grown in the tropics—two hundred varieties of palm trees, more than five hundred different orchids, uncounted fragrant flowering trees, beds of hibiscus, cannas, and bushes of the diefenbachia and philodendron we nurture as house plants. We lost track of the colors of bougainvillea.

It was impossible to take in all 150 acres, like seeing too many paintings in an art gallery. We did what we could, stopping to rest at gazebos, pavilions, benches, and a restaurant where a delicious fruit drink—pineapple, mango, papaya, and banana—revived us.

Mark Twain also found Sri Lanka a perfect feast for the eye:

> What a dream it was of tropical splendors of bloom and blossom, and Oriental conflagrations of costume! The walking groups of men, women, boys, girls, babies—each individual was a flame, each group a house afire for color. And such stunning colors, such intensely vivid colors, such rich and exquisite minglings and fusings of rainbows and lightnings! And all harmonious, all in perfect taste; never a discordant note; never a color on any person swearing at another color on him or failing to harmonize faultlessly with the colors of any group the wearer might join. The stuffs were silk—thin, soft, delicate, clinging; and, as a rule, each piece a solid color: a splendid green, a splendid blue, a splendid yellow, a splendid purple, a splendid ruby, deep and rich with smouldering fires—they swept continuously by in crowds and legions and multitudes, glowing, flashing, burning, radiant; and every five seconds came a burst of a blinding red that made a

body catch his breath and filled his heart with joy.
And then, the unimaginable grace of those costumes!
Sometimes a woman's whole dress was but a scarf
wound about her person and her head, sometimes a
man's was but a turban and a careless rag or two—
in both cases generous areas of polished dark skin
showing—but always the arrangement compelled
the homage of the eye and made the heart sing for
gladness.

That was all very pretty. But there were snakes in this
Eden. Or rather, worms.

In the early years of this century Dr. Victor Heiser,
director for the East of the International Health Board
and associated with the Rockefeller Foundation, took on
the colonial establishment of Ceylon in a public health
battle of extraordinary proportions. Sent to the island by
the foundation in 1915 to demonstrate the beneficial
results of hookworm control, a project dear to the heart
of John D. Rockefeller, Dr. Heiser determined that soil
pollution was a major problem. Before he could tackle it,
however, he had to contend with the tea planters who
imported Tamil laborers from India to do the work that
native-born Sinhalese chose not to do. The planters wanted
no interference from health authorities and contended
that "nothing can be done with Tamils."

Next, the good doctor took on the colonial government
which had its own health agency and did not want Yankees
challenging its efficiency or authority. Finally, he had to
contend with Tamil superstition and the enmity of traditional herbalists. By persistence he at last secured permission to demonstrate on a small number of tea estates
the effectiveness of capsules of oil of chenopodium as a
cure, and the use of latrines for prevention of infection.
The results were dramatic. Sickness and absenteeism
dropped immediately.

Planters continued to protest that Tamils would not

use latrines, but Heiser undertook to instruct the laborers on latrine use and purpose. He enforced compliance with fines for dereliction. It was not long before the methods spread to other estates and by 1921 two hundred thousand people had been freed of hookworm. In time the number of Tamils imported from India was reduced because the work force was not being depleted by illness and death, and the women, no longer suffering from anemia, began to bear healthy children.

It could be argued that Dr. Heiser's health measures are responsible for today's civil war in Sri Lanka. Longstanding animosity permeates the relationship between Sinhalese and Tamils. Seven out of ten Sri Lankans are Sinhalese Buddhists whose ancestors migrated from north India many centuries ago. The rest are Tamil Hindus from south India, many of whom are "Ceylon Tamils" whose forebears came from south India generations ago and who are entitled to be considered natives. But almost half the Tamils are imported laborers. Racial differences are exacerbated by language problems and religious differences. Basically the charming, smiling Sinhalese and the dour, hardworking Tamils just plain don't like each other.

The Tamils claim discrimination in jobs, language, education, and basic rights, and are demanding creation of a separate state in the north. The Sinhalese, in spite of their Buddhist belief in forgiveness of enemies and friendliness to all, apparently do not include the Tamils. In the business district of Colombo we saw the blackened remains of Tamil business buildings that had been looted and burned the previous year.

Today civil war has taken over the Island of Serendip. Discriminatory legislation, in a country that since independence in 1948 had maintained a functioning parliamentary democracy, led to a nationwide explosion and widespread rioting in July 1983. Faced with a system unwilling to provide for their livelihood or even protect their lives, the Tamil population has joined with Marxist guerrillas.

On July 29, 1987, an Indo-Sri Lankan peace accord allowed some fifty thousand Indian troops to be stationed on the island to prevent violence between the majority Sinhalese and minority Tamils. Two years after they entered the country, supposedly to safeguard Sri Lanka's three million Tamils, the Indian troops had suffered more than a thousand deaths fighting the guerrillas. The conflict continues. There seems to be no solution.

A Sinhalese friend writes us: "It is no longer safe here." Events have given the lie to the tourist board brochure we received, proclaiming: "The Buddhist doctrine of peace and tolerance has left its gentle mark on the land and her people. Different religions and ethnic groups live side by side in total harmony in a democratic society which strives today to establish the unique concept of a Free and Just Society."

The drive from the highlands south to the seacoast opened up a whole new geography. The mountains were rolling, rounded, graceful curves, green with prolific vegetation and usually softened further by a caressing mist. Here the tea plantations are laid out as though by a landscape gardener, artistically peopled by Tamil women in brilliant costumes picking only the youngest, tenderest leaves from each stem. It was at a tea plantation here that we learned that the name Orange Pekoe has nothing to do with oranges, but refers to the color of the tea leaves.

In the valleys and up the mountain slopes it seemed that every foot where a farmer could get purchase was terraced and farmed. Vegetables grew in orderly rows in every swale. Every piece of ground not cultivated was taken over by forest and vine. Villages—a few huts and shops of bamboo—rose every mile or so, with isolated thatched cottages in between. Profusions of bougainvillea festooned every humble hut. Hibiscus and flame-of-the-forest blazed across the valleys and through the mists. Dramatic waterfalls and forests came into view and vanished. We passed through rubber plantations and saw a group of children, drenched from the rain, bouncing huge balls of raw rubber. I would have loved to stop and buy one, but our suitcases were becoming ever heavier and I knew that we had about exhausted both space and muscle.

At Bandarawela, a health resort at seven thousand feet "where it is always spring," we met some of the last remaining British people in Sri Lanka at a colonial hostel. The husband manages one of the few foreign-owned operations not nationalized after independence. From him we got the British view that the spice gardens and tea and rubber plantations have suffered continuing deterioration under management by local political appointees without qualifications or experience. Exports of these products drop significantly year by year as root stock and trees are not replanted or properly maintained.

"President Junius Richard Jayewardene hoped to make Sri Lanka another Singapore," he told us. "The problem is that you can't make a Singapore without the Chinese. Here you never know on any working day how many people will report for work. If they have enough rice for a day or two, they are satisfied. Buddhism is not conducive to ambition. The people are able, reasonably industrious, and easily trained. The problem is that any who learn skills and are ambitious can earn more money in the Middle East. So they're off. Next to tea, the largest income-producer of Sri Lanka is remittances."

The road to the seacoast from Bandarawela was a horror, made worse by intermittent rain and drifting fog.

The soil was saturated from monsoon rains. (Sri Lanka has two monsoons; this was the minor one.) Giant boulders, trees, and sections of rice paddies and tea plantations had been swept onto the highway at frequent intervals from the uphill side, and there were no barriers or warning signs. On the downhill side were cave-ins, washouts, and rivulets, and the crumbling remains of blacktop overhung precipitous drop-offs into intensively farmed valleys. Jaya held the wheel with aplomb, steering around obstructions and skirting the edges of wash-outs. He never once stopped to test the surface.

We passed a procession of Buddhist monks accompanied by drummers and carriers of banners. "What do they say?" we asked Jaya. "The signs say, 'Stop the killing, all Lankans are our brothers.' " It was a peace march that would walk the whole length of Sri Lanka.

Whether they like each other or not, the most resplendent asset of the Resplendent Land is its resplendent people. With a literacy rate of 86 percent and life expectancy of sixty-eight years, Sri Lanka is unique in Asia. It has a lot going for it. Life in the Sinhalese coastal villages we saw was a joyous celebration. Schoolgirls in their starched white emerged giggling from school, boys played soccer, and amazingly beautiful women walked singly or in groups.

Those women! Winston was enchanted. Young and old, they walked with a fine, upright carriage, trim-waisted, slim-hipped, their small, firm breasts molded into their close-fitting choli blouses. The sarong, knotted at the hip, becomes them wonderfully. We never saw a fat one. We never saw a crone. Older women had the same elegant stride as their daughters. A study should be undertaken to measure the estrogen levels of Sinhalese women. Moreover, they were immaculately groomed. Heavy black hair, drawn into a ballerina knot, framed their café-au-lait faces. Their children were predictably pretty with large eyes and white teeth.

The Sinhalese are big on processions. We passed a procession of mourners making their way to the funeral of a Buddhist holy man, processions for weddings and for religious holidays, and perhaps even just for fun. From every doorway, hanging from archways and poles and altars fell soft, pale yellow streamers made of young coconut palm leaves, an effective and appropriate local adornment and just one more manifestation of the usefulness of the coconut tree. It yields meat, milk, oil, fuel, sugar, syrup, toddy, and thatch. Husk fibers are woven into rope. One or several coconut trees are often the dowry of a bride. As we drove through the jungle in the late afternoon, the smell of coconut permeated the air. Coconut milk is the liquid for the evening curry.

Unlike our original drive from Colombo along the western seacoast, this highway (I use the term loosely) along the southern tip of Sri Lanka skirted the Indian Ocean and sandy beaches. Gentle, rolling waves—not the high surf of Hawaii or the rocky and roiling backwaters of Fiji—invited swimmers and fishermen. The air was humid and steamy and we had the feeling that Sri Lanka might have been the primeval stew of the beginning of the world.

Our bodies and our sensibilities were tired from all the sights, sounds, smells, and sensations. We stopped at a beautiful, quiet villa on Bentota Beach. It was small, elegantly furnished, and had only six guests. After a fine dinner we fell asleep listening to the waves washing on the shore. In the morning we swam in the Indian Ocean and lay in the sun on the sand. It was good not to see a single Buddha. After six days and five nights on the road, returning to the Cinnamon Gardens Inn was like coming home. Sri Lanka was the furthest point from home in our travels.

CHAPTER VIII

South Africa's Tide Is Coming In

The great bulk of the savages must go. The white man wants their lands, and all must go excepting such percentage of them as he will need to do his work for him upon terms to be determined by himself. Since history has removed the element of guesswork from this matter and made it certainty, the humanest way of diminishing the black population should be adopted, not the old cruel ways of the past. Mr. Rhodes and his gang have been following the old ways. They are chartered to rob and slay, and they lawfully do it, but not in a compassionate and Christian spirit.

Mark Twain

Seen from the air, the shore of Africa was outlined with white surf which made it look remarkably like a map. Our destination, Johannesburg, was far inland.

After two weeks of the sea level humidity and equatorial languor of Sri Lanka and a week with friends in the Seychelles, the five-thousand-foot altitude of Johannesburg snapped us back to reality. Mark Twain had long sea voyages between countries, and journeys by rail inland from seacoasts onto high plateaus to adjust gradually to changes. We underwent atmospheric shock. It was like suddenly being in Denver or Butte. The air was tangy, cool, bracing. This country, unlike Bangladesh, India, and Sri Lanka, meant business.

The taxi driver could have been from New York. He saw few Americans and seemed glad to unburden himself of his opinions: he liked what he saw of America on television but wouldn't want to live there. It's too dangerous. "You have a much worse problem with the blacks than we do. You've tried to integrate with them and live with them. Now, you can't do that. A black man isn't like a white man. A black man's wealth is his wives and children. A white man's wealth is his money. A black man has ten wives and has children by all of them. The white man can't keep up. They'll take over. Yes, they'll take over, but they won't run things. They know they've got it good here. They're good blacks. But they stink. God, how they stink. Haven't you noticed? But we know we can't live with them like you Americans think you can."

There was a sign on the door of the Italian restaurant where we had dinner: "We reserve the right to select our customers." It did not say, "Whites Only." Soon we were sharing a bottle of wine with three Belgians at an adjoining table—a chef, an electrical engineer, and a hair stylist—who freely discussed their reasons for migrating to South Africa, their prospects here, the local wines; recommended choices on the Italian menu; and offered their opinions of apartheid.

They had few regrets. "There's nothing back home for us," they concluded. "And the climate there is rotten."

As to the future of South Africa, they hoped for the best. It was apparently an ongoing source of discussion and argument among the three friends. They agreed that apartheid would go, but were unsure what would take its place. There would not be a revolution, they were quite sure. In the meantime, they kept their Belgian passports. The hair stylist, the most analytical and vocal of the three, set high hopes on the ascendancy of the *Egoli*, the emerging young, educated black professionals. Diners came and went. No blacks sought entrance.

SOUTH AFRICA'S TIDE IS COMING IN

Our German son-in-law had sent word of our visit to his relatives in Johannesburg and Cape Town. These families had left Germany for South Africa after World War II; introductions to them gave us access to a cross-section of South African society and opinion not readily available to travellers, and a chance to enjoy South African hospitality. A telephone call to Helmut and Anna von Schach, our German "relatives," elicited an immediate invitation for cocktails and we were soon picked up by Helmut, a tall, handsome businessman driving a Mercedes.

Their suburban home was a spacious colonial house in a walled-in compound with a swimming pool and a wide verandah, from which we watched the sun set behind what appeared to be distant hills. We learned later that they were old gold mine dumps. Our host and his wife held to the liberal, anti-apartheid views of most educated foreigners. Another guest, also of German extraction, held the opposite views. "Of course you'll be mugged," he commented upon hearing that we were staying in a commercial hotel near the railroad station. Our hosts derided him. We weren't mugged.

A neighbor, a ninth-generation Afrikaner, out walking his dog, dropped in. A prominent Johannesburg lawyer and businessman, he was entertaining, knowledgeable, and outspokenly bigoted. He pointed out to us that his family had come to South Africa only thirty-two years after the pilgrims landed in Massachusetts. "We've been here longer than the blacks. We've settled them in their own homelands and spent a lot of money for their education and welfare. In fact, we have here the world's largest foreign aid program. Look around you. You'll see what we've done with this country. We aren't about to give it up." (That whites have been in South Africa longer than blacks is often claimed, but untrue.)

A spur-of-the-moment dinner party was arranged at

an authentic Afrikaans restaurant furnished with *voortrekker* (literally forward trekker, akin to our western pioneers) antiques. After our many weeks of rice and curry, we found the Boer food heavy.

It was agreed that we must witness the performance to be given by gold miners the next morning—competitive teams of miners from four mines demonstrating their tribal dances and costumes. It was athletic, to say the least, with much foot stomping and leaping. Some dances were humorous mimes. One group wore tin cans filled with pebbles on their legs, creating percussion accompaniment. There were suggestive shimmiers with brass bells on bodices. The star of the show was a stand-out shimmier, who played wildly to the crowd with absolute joy, spontaneity, and humor. The dancing resembled that of American Indians, also strong on stomping and drumming. But the Blackfeet Indians, with whom we are familiar, are much more restrained, sober, and dignified. Indians dance with purpose, usually religious, while these miners seemed to dance from sheer exuberance.

Walking along a Johannesburg street I observed a young black woman call to three men lounging on a corner. She hailed them with a song in a rich contralto. The three answered her in a harmonic blending of voices, which ended when she joined them to hilarious laughter and hand-clapping. We were startled when a pretty young black woman, attractively dressed and wearing high heels, passed us on the street carrying a large suitcase on her head. No one else seemed to notice.

Our hotel allowed black guests, so said a sign over the registration desk. There was an occasional black in the elevator and in the dining room. I watched one young man dressed in a business suit eat a hard roll with a knife and fork, and was unable to tell him that this was not required.

Several (white) South Africans told us that, except

SOUTH AFRICA'S TIDE IS COMING IN

for color, American black people bear no resemblance to their South African counterparts. "You can spot them in a minute," one told me. "How?" I asked. "By the way they walk." And by the way they speak: an Afrikaans woman told of walking down the street followed by three American sailors conversing in "that peculiar American accent." When she turned around she was shocked to discover that one was black. "Why," she said, "it was simply uncanny. They talked just alike. You really couldn't tell them apart from their speech." By contrast, black South Africans grow up with English as a second or even a third language, and usually speak it with a strong accent.

The Johannesburg *Star*, the leading English-language newspaper, published a series of articles by a four-man investigating team entitled: "The New Egoli—Black Society in the Year 2000." *Egoli*, meaning the place of gold, originally referred to Johannesburg. The *Star* used it to fill the linguistic vacuum to describe the newly emerging black middle class. It means achievement, relative wealth, urbanization, and upward mobility.

Blacks resent the term middle class. How, they want to know, can you have a middle class when you have no upper class? It also implies an inclination among black people to mimic white westerners and turn their backs on their black identity. A black doctor quoted in the series said, "A middle class without the vote is ridiculous because it is members of that class who should not only manage the professions but also be active in local government and in Parliament."

For more than a hundred years black workers from rural areas have been coming to the cities for jobs. By 1982 one-third of black urban households had incomes of more than four hundred rand (about two hundred dollars) a month, while only a handful of rural households had such an income, indicating an enormous difference in standards of living.

THE POLITICAL POT

SOUTH AFRICA'S TIDE IS COMING IN

Black society is growing new upper strata of doctors, dentists, lawyers, degreed nurses, and high school teachers, managers, sales representatives, and trained businessmen and women. In black "townships" and white cities, these people are employed in a full range of enterprises. They have begun to drive European and Japanese cars, and own television sets, refrigerators, and electric stoves. This level of affluence is usually dependent on two incomes in *Monna ga a loale* homes—translated, "the husband cannot take ill." The implied other half of this is "and the wife may not fall pregnant."

The study divided black society into four categories: the motivated, the frustrated, the traditional, and the swingers. The egoli are those catagorized as motivated. The growing importance of South Africa's blacks as consumers is an aspect that has apparently dawned slowly on some local economists. An estimated 9.5 percent of cars are now owned by black people, who make up 80 percent of the population. One out of every two whites now owns a car. The market is saturated. The hope is that by the end of the century, the ratio of car ownership among blacks might be the same as for whites. I don't know where they're going to park them in ticky-tacky, crackerbox communities like Soweto, Johannesburg's huge black satellite.

Whites brag that seventy-four thousand Soweto houses were wired for electricity; but the cost of hooking them up to power was so high that only seven thousand actually used electricity. Perhaps there will eventually be a huge demand for electric stoves, refrigerators, and hi-fi sets. Inevitably, higher incomes and better education will groom growing numbers of black families to be consumers.

In the meantime, a leading black businessman educated in Britain and the United States sums it up: "Whether you are a doctor, lawyer, business executive, teacher, or any other professional, you are stopped on the street by policemen demanding your pass. You are forced to strip naked at the pass office the same way as anyone else. And whether you own a house like I do or not, every year you have to return to your town of origin to obtain permission to stay in your house in the city. So where is this middle class?"

I showed Helmut von Schach Mark Twain's description of a Boer:

> He is deeply religious, profoundly ignorant, dull, obstinate, bigoted, uncleanly in his habits, hospitable, honest in his dealings with the whites, a hard master to his black servant, lazy, a good shot, good horseman, addicted to the chase, a lover of political independence, a good husband and father, not fond of herding together in towns, but liking the seclusion and remoteness and solitude and empty vastness and silence of the veldt; a man of mighty appetite, and not delicate about what he appeases it with ... requiring only that the quantity shall not be stinted, willing to ride a long journey to take a hand in a rude all-night dance interspersed with vigorous feeding and boisterous jollity, but ready to ride twice as far for a prayer-meeting; proud of his Dutch and Huguenot origin and its religious and military history; proud of his race's achievements in South Africa, its bold plunges into hostile and unchartered deserts in search of free solitudes unvested by the pestering and detested English, also its victories over the natives and the British; proudest of all of the direct and personal interest which the Deity has always taken in its affairs. He cannot read, he cannot write; ... until latterly he had no schools, and taught his children nothing. ... He has stood stock still in South Africa for two centuries and a half and would like to stand still till the end of time. ... Now what would you expect from that unpromising material? ... The Uitlander seems to have expected something very different. ... I do

> not know why. Nothing different from it was ratio-
> nally to be expected. A round man cannot be expected
> to fit into a square hole right away. He must have
> time to modify his shape.

Helmut had not seen this before and he laughed. But he is optimistic that the Boers may have had time to "modify their shape." Although he has lived, studied, and worked here most of his life, Helmut has thought deeply about the problem of apartheid. He wrote his doctoral thesis at a Swiss university under the forbidding title: "Developmental Politics in the South African Republic: Positive and Negative Experience and Knowledge."

"Bigots and racists are becoming more of a minority. More and more whites are recognizing the justice of black demands," he told me. He offered this original insight:

"When we talk about integration we mean integration *our* way. What's wrong with integration *their* way? Look at black society. It is rooted in an ancient and stable tradition of loving and dependable family ties and caring for each other—all of which they are sure of. Yes, it's true what you heard that a brilliant young man educated at a foreign university might go back to his tribe and herd cattle. But what you don't understand—what we don't understand—is that he would do this gladly, willingly, unquestioningly, and it would not be difficult for him to adjust to this. His first duty is to his family and to his tribe. If we did this, it would cause a breakdown. But not for him. And he will be happy.

"Look what is happening to the Japanese. Look at their suicide rate and mental breakdowns. They have made a complete change in their lifestyle to achieve prosperity and industrialization. At what cost?" For the first time I had some understanding of university-educated Montana Indians returning to tribal life. We call it "going back to the blanket."

AFTER YOU, MARK TWAIN

Back in our hotel room we read the Johannesburg *Star* and watched television. A man and woman sang the songs of Gershwin, Kern, Sigmund Romberg. The *Star* reported: " 'Dallas,' now nearing the end of its run on TV1, has regained the No. 1 spot in the television popularity stakes. The latest survey put 'Dallas' on top with 'Private Benjamin' second, the Afrikaans soapie 'Fynbos' third and 'Star Trek' holding its own in fourth position."

All visitors to South Africa feel obligated to visit the vast game sanctuary, the Kruger National Park, some 250 miles northeast of Johannesburg. Since it was not established as a game reserve until after Mark Twain's visit to the country, he missed it. Mario Godden, a knowledgeable Swede, was our courier for a three-day trek in a microbus with a dozen assorted tourists, among them a college professor and his wife, recently returned from leading an antarctic cruise from Christchurch to Cape Town.

It was a poor time to spot game. After a long drought, the rains had come. High grass hid the animals, and they no longer clustered at familiar water holes. We saw only one elephant, a few giraffes, herds of zebras, wildebeest, springbok, and warthogs. Jammed bang up against Mozambique along its eastern border and Zimbabwe on the north, the Kruger Park is the size of Massachusetts. Mario told us that if we drove all day every day for ten days we would see only 10 percent of the park. It is home to some eight thousand elephants.

The most interesting fauna were the birds, luminescent, enterprising, and industrious. Nests of weaver birds hung like Christmas tree ornaments from riverside trees. Nests are made by the male, but frequently fail to pass the inspection of the female, who scorns substandard structures, rips them apart, and leaves them shredded and empty to twist in the wind. The incompetent male then proceeds to build another, and another, until he makes one that passes muster.

The names of South African birds sound as if they were invented by Dr. Seuss: secretary bird, ground hornbill, lilac-breasted roller, carmine bee eater, marabou stork, kori bustard, long-tailed widow, malachite sunbird, bald ibis, red-billed oxpecker, purple-crested loerie, and the sugarbirds, which live from and pollinate that botanical extravaganza, the South African protea. I was most impressed with the secretary bird, a large, no-nonsense fowl with what appears to be a quill pen protruding from its head.

I rather begrudged the time spent on this safari, but had we not taken it, we would have missed seeing the richness and variety of the Transvaal Province. Outside Johannesburg we passed miles of waste dumps from the gold mines which have provided a century's work for black laborers, digging out the ore by the shovelful and carrying the leavings here to make these mountains; the cooling towers of a coal-fired power plant and the coal mine that fed it; great fields of wheat and corn, changing as we lost altitude to bananas, coconuts, and citrus fruits; plantations of eucalyptus and pine; pastures with sheep and cattle, each acreage allotted its optimum use. The landscape was orderly and productive. Almost too orderly. No house, barn, machine shed, or clutter of outbuildings indicated a farm. Nobody seemed to live here. The absence of human activity was eerie. There was not so much as a cloud of dust on the horizon where someone on a tractor might be cultivating. There was no sign of anyone fixing a fence or irrigating or pruning or visiting with a neighbor. The Transvaal is agribusiness. It was clear why so many black people must flock to the cities.

We returned to Johannesburg along backcountry roads, snaking through steep valleys where goldseekers had panned the gravel of the streams, tunneled into the sidehills, and died of disease and hunger. We stopped for lunch at the restored mining town of Pilgrim's Rest. We passed a tribal homeland: squalor, poverty, and hopelessness. Still visible are the ruts of the ox-wagons driven by the voortrekkers who settled and tamed this wilderness.

We flew from Johannesburg to Cape Town, landing at Bloemfontein and Kimberley, passing over the Kimberley diamond crater. Known as the Big Hole, it offered diggers a brief free-for-all before Cecil Rhodes and the DeBeers Consolidated Mining Company bought up small claims to form a conglomerate still dominant in diamond mining today. In 1910 South Africa produced more than 98 percent of the world's diamonds.

Mark Twain was so intrigued with diamond mining that he could hardly turn loose of it.

> The gold fields are wonderful in every way. ... I had been a gold miner myself, in my day, and knew substantially everything that those people knew about it, except how to make money at it ... but the diamond mine was a wholly fresh thing, a splendid and absorbing novelty. ... The pasturage covering the surface of the Kimberley crater was sufficient for the support of a cow, and the pasturage underneath was sufficient for the support of a kingdom; but the cow did not know it, and lost her chance. The Kimberley crater is roomy enough to admit the Roman coliseum.

He speculated about early discoveries, musing that diamonds must always have been lying around on the surface, and "you would think that they would have been valued by the natives almost as much as a glass bead." But it apparently did not occur to them to try to sell them to whites, because, of course "the whites already had plenty

146

of glass beads, and more fashionably shaped, too, than these; but one would think that the poorer sort of black, who could not afford real glass, would have been humbly content to decorate himself with the imitation." One black man, however, did hit the jackpot, as Twain recorded:

> Some years ago ... a black found what has been claimed to be the largest diamond known to the world's history; and as a reward he was released from service and given a blanket, a horse, and $500. It made him a Vanderbilt. He could buy four wives, and have money left. ...
> That great diamond weighs 971 carats. Some say it is as big as a piece of alum, others say it is as large as a bite of rock candy, but the best authorities

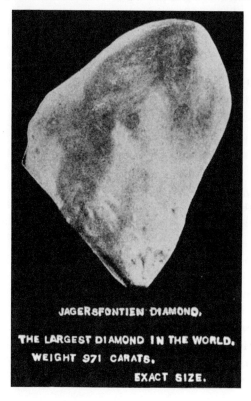

JAGERSFONTIEN DIAMOND,

THE LARGEST DIAMOND IN THE WORLD,

WEIGHT 971 CARATS,

EXACT SIZE.

> agree that it is almost exactly the size of a chunk of
> ice. ... It is owned by a syndicate, and apparently
> there is no satisfactory market for it. It is earning
> nothing; it is eating its head off. Up to this time it
> has made nobody rich but the native who found it.

The whole inland territory bordering the Kalahari desert appeared from the air to be swept by dust storms, a desolate waste, good for nothing but mining asbestos and diamonds. Called the *Karoo*, place of great dryness, it is home to most of South Africa's sheep. Nearing the coast, we began to see mountains, rocky, unwooded ridges, sand in the valleys, occasional settlements, and finally the Atlantic Ocean, ruffling the coast with the same maplike definition as the Indian Ocean had given it on the east.

Mark Twain made the proper approach to Cape Town—by ship. It is a dramatic setting for a city. Table Mountain looms like a stage-set cut from cardboard. Today highrises cluster near the harbor but are relieved by a cobbled square and greenery to provide breathing space. Botanical gardens and parks and storybook houses of Cape Dutch design, each in its own carefully groomed flower garden, make the city an artistic masterpiece.

The Cape of Good Hope is the most southerly tip of the African continent. The Portuguese explorer Diaz was the first European to come upon it. That was in 1488. Vasco da Gama sailed past it on his way to India in 1498. Early mariners had called it the Cape of Storms, but Sir Francis Drake, headed home after circumnavigating the globe, wrote in his ship's log: "This Cape is a most stately thing, and the fairest we saw in the whole circumference of the earth."

Jan van Riebeeck was sent to the Cape by the Dutch East India Company in 1652 to establish a "hospital and victualling station" to provide for ship crews on their voyages between the Netherlands and the East Indies. It had become customary for company ships to land at Table Bay for rest and recreation of their sailors, as many as half of whom died on those long voyages. Here they took on fresh water and bartered with little brown people with clicking speech—Hottentots—for sheep and oxen to provide meat for their onward voyages.

It wasn't long before Van Riebeeck's supply depot was surrounded by farms and orchards. Fruit, to combat the sailors' scurvy, was high on the list of necessaries. Today every imaginable fruit, from apples to mangoes, grows somewhere in South Africa. Van Riebeeck himself imported the first cuttings of grape vines from Germany, being of the opinion that civilization goes with wine and wine with civilization. The soil was poor, the sun was hot—perfect conditions for grapes. The arrival of French Huguenots brought the art of wine-making. Excellent wine has resulted.

The Cape Province seems, perhaps even more than Sri Lanka, a veritable Eden. But here a line from Anglican Bishop Heber's missionary hymn has bearing: "Where every prospect pleases, and only man is vile." Mark Twain also recognized the contradiction: "We reached Cape Town and the end of our African journeyings. And well satisfied; for towering above us was Table Mountain—a reminder that we had now seen each and all of the great features of South Africa except Mr. Cecil Rhodes. ... The whole South African world seemed to stand in a kind of shuddering awe of him, friend and enemy alike. ... I admire him, I frankly confess it; and when his time comes I shall buy a piece of the rope for a keepsake."

Here in this country of compulsory military service, a mother said, "Do you think our son is going to join up and kill his own people?" Sadly, another woman confided to me, "My children will have to leave. There is no future for them here."

AFTER YOU, MARK TWAIN

Why? The chief thing lacking if there is to be harmony is consultation between the rulers and the ruled. The ruling Afrikaners number 3.5 million, the blacks between twenty-one million and twenty-three million. The black population is growing at the rate of thirty per thousand, the whites at 8.2 per thousand. The fear is of being overwhelmed by black numbers—suicide, according to the Afrikaners. It is a real fear. But their solution of concentrating total power into their own hands, rather than working out some system of power-sharing with the black majority, has failed. By preventing most contact between blacks and whites—residence, marriage, sex, politics, entertainment, sports, even toilets, elevators, waiting lines, buses, trains, restaurants—the system of apartheid has made interracial friendships rare, and has fostered fear and revulsion.

The Afrikaners should be able to survive. They have a viable language, literature, culture, religion, history, identity. They are tremendously talented and capable. But could even they, with all their talent and energy, make a living on the 13 percent of the poorest land in South Africa to which they have consigned so many black people?

We Americans, busy casting stones at the Afrikaners, might consider our own history. In short order, American settlers rid themselves of the "Indian problem" by smallpox, guns, whiskey, and killing off the buffalo. After that the nagging problem of land ownership was handily dispatched by revocation of any treaties inconvenient to whites, and by pushing tribes onto reservations. If it turned out that reservation land proved desirable, by changing a few laws, whites could crowd onto that land by leasing, buying, or outright chicanery.

South Africa's indigenous population was not thus decimated, however; laborers were needed for mines and

farms, and numbers of settlers were small. On the streets
of Cape Town we were impressed by black women, with
contented infants fastened on their backs by blanket and
safety pin. They moved about the city in clusters of five or
ten, conversing in liquid and mellow voices, window-
shopping, and laughing, I suspected, at the discomfort of
whites. South African blacks seemed to us conspicuously
vigorous, robust, and healthy. They are not about to die
out. Whatever the Afrikaners may command, the tide is
coming in.

Angelika Flegg, a sister of Helmut von Schach, picked
us up early on a Sunday morning to show us Cape Town.
It was something to see. Up the side of a mountain to a
splendid overlook of the town, the harbor, and Table
Mountain; past the dignified buildings of the University
of Cape Town; past Groote Schuur Hospital where the
first heart transplant was performed; past innumerable
parks, pink seaside hotels flanked by tennis courts and

swimming pools in manicured grounds; and a bulldozed scar where a black shantytown had been leveled and its inhabitants removed, "endorsed," outside the city.

"Where to?" we asked. "Who knows?" she replied. "It was terribly sad and there was a big outcry over it. Of course it was a slum, full of rats and vermin and it needed to be cleaned up. I just don't know ..."

Angelika, a big, handsome woman of about fifty, mother of four, has strong moral convictions. She disapproves of the South African government and has taken a job teaching English and German at a black college. I inquired about her approach to teaching. "It's a combination of wheedling and threatening," she answered. "Plus never compromising." Also involved is a real attempt to understand the demands of the black culture—the compelling necessity for students to return to their villages for funerals, rituals, festivities. "These are, to them, legitimate excuses. They simply must be accepted," she explained. There's no question but that black education is terribly neglected, she said. South Africa spends much less on the education of a black child than on a white one. This applies down the line from teacher preparation to school buildings and textbooks.

To give us an idea of the charismatic Christianity which is sweeping the country, Angelika took us to a two-hour Baptist service. It seemed a conventional church to us with good singing by both congregation and choir, and a well-reasoned sermon by the minister. Then, without preface, a man and a woman rose and spoke intensely and at length in a foreign language, which we took to be Afrikaans. It turned out that they were speaking in tongues! They never seemed to be at a loss for words, and the congregation paid rapt attention. I asked Angelika if she understood them. She said she didn't. The seriousness of the two and their apparent conviction were disconcerting. The man was spectacularly handsome. The woman placed a scarf over her head before she began. We felt as though we were witnessing a performance. When I told Angelika that this was a whole new experience for us, she laughed and said that she could have taken us to a much more dramatic service but figured we might not be equal to it. The charismatic movement is seen in several faiths, and it is widely believed that only through Christ's love can a peaceful solution to South Africa's troubles be found. It is a hope and a refuge from fear and despair.

Sunday dinner with Angelika's extended family in a much-lived-in house on a middle-class street had an energetic atmosphere. At the table, in addition to her husband, four children and spouses of the elder three, were a baby grandson, a niece from Germany, a sister-in-law who is an authority on African languages, and two handsome young Argentinian university students, one of whom was courting the Fleggs' youngest daughter. (Buenos Aires is 3,776 nautical miles from Cape Town.) A weeping black woman waited in the drive to talk with Angelika. We never learned of her problem.

The Villa Lutzi, a lovely bed and breakfast home where Angelika had arranged for us to stay, was overbooked with Germans. Our host loaded us and our luggage into his Mercedes and moved us further up the beautiful street to a comfortable, cluttered two-story Victorian house full of bric-a-brac and antique furniture. Every room had a fireplace. Here our host was justice of the supreme court.

Also a guest there was a woman who had been a missionary nurse in Rhodesia and South Africa for twenty years. She had returned from her home in England to visit our hosts, who had been members of her hospital board when she was supervisor of a maternity hospital in Cape

Town. Hers was perhaps the most objective and sympathetic analysis of the South African dilemma that we heard.

She had gone to Rhodesia (now Zimbabwe) as a nurse at a Salvation Army mission when she was just out of training. In the absence of a doctor, she found herself transformed overnight into a practicing physician, diagnosing and treating all manner of diseases and injuries in a black community. This was in addition to recruiting and training black nurses, her original assignment. She found the nurses both competent and devoted. When the end of her tour came, she was reluctant to return to being an ordinary nursing sister; she loved Africa, and going home "would have been terribly boring," she said.

She moved to Cape Town into a job as a hospital supervisor. Discovering that some of the white nurses—better paid than their black aides—were incompetent, poorly trained, and lazy, she instead hired and promoted black nurses. The hospital was running very well when she received a call from the director of another Cape Town hospital, asking to know the secret of her effective administration. She told him. There was a long pause. Finally he said, "Forget that you ever told me this." And hung up.

"I have spent my life trying to foster change," she told me. "I see a great change in South Africa since I left. It won't be the same violent change as in Zimbabwe. The Afrikaners are too strong and too well organized for that. But the final change will come when the present generation of older Afrikaners are gone. Then the rigidity will vanish. The young people are better educated and have broader experience than their parents. They do not share their parents' ideas. This is causing great friction between the generations. They feel that leadership should be on the basis of intelligence and ability, not skin color. Change is coming. If the blacks will only wait, the change will come peacefully in the next generation."

She is not unaware of the hazards involved in turning administrative responsibilities over to people who aren't ready for them. When a Zimbabwean was given command of her former station, the tradition of family loyalty took precedence and it became impossible for him to function dependably, she told us. Because of his position he was expected to give handouts to all family members who presented themselves. This enigma was seconded by a prominent Afrikaans woman who pointed out that whites simply don't recognize the demands on a successful black man. "He is besieged by a horde of relatives who expect and demand his support."

At the judge's home, the maid served us delicious breakfasts of beautiful fruits, hot breads, and coddled eggs on elegant bone china. When we thanked her she replied humbly, "It is my privilege." It made us uncomfortable. We lingered over breakfast with the judge one morning. Highly educated, widely travelled, and thoroughly Afrikaans, the judge, who is also a successful farmer, reiterated that the whites of the Republic of South Africa rightfully consider this their motherland. He concluded, "Yes, there will be change and movement toward bringing the coloreds and blacks into the government. It will be slow, I hope, but it's got to come. But there's no way that one man, one vote can work in this country which is 80 percent black."

His wife, equally adamant if not more so, told me, "We Afrikaners have our religion and our courage. We will die here. Have you read Alan Paton?" When I admitted that I had read work by this distinguished liberal and novelist, she said, "Alan Paton hates South Africa."

AFTER YOU, MARK TWAIN

Wherever we went we had looked for evidence that Mark Twain had been there before us. There was no question but that the "celebrated American author," the "greatest humorist of the age," the "star of the Stars and Stripes" had captivated the British colonies. Samuel Clemens's "At Homes" had the happy result of making his guests feel at home, as well. Although he claimed to have "robbed and raided" on his route along the equator, when he sidled off those hundreds of stages in his dress suit, he left behind audiences who were the better for laughter, and who felt they had gotten their money's worth. He also left behind a favorable image of an American.

The Clemenses and their daughter enjoyed the hospitality of important homes wherever they went. Just before leaving Cape Town, while at dinner at an old Dutch mansion, Mark Twain saw "a picture of a pale, intellectual young man in a pink coat with a high black collar." This chance glimpse led him to tell the story of a "curious romance," that of Dr. James Barry, a military surgeon who had come to the Cape fifty years earlier with his regiment. A wild young man, apparently impervious to the wiles of pretty girls, Barry was frequently reported, but never officially reprimanded for misbehavior.

Instead, he was promoted and transferred to India. Soon he returned to the Cape and to his old escapades. Once he was called for a hopeless case of a woman believed to be dying in childbirth. He saved both mother and child. His reputation as a physician was only exceeded by his reputation as a rakehell.

"The story seems to be arriving nowhere," Mark Twain concluded. "But that is because I have not finished. Dr. Barry died in Cape Town 30 years ago. It was then discovered that he was a *woman*.

"The legend goes that inquiries—soon silenced—developed the fact that she was a daughter of a great

English house, and that that was why her Cape wildnesses brought no punishment and got no notice when reported to the government at home. Her name was an alias. She had disgraced herself with her people; so she chose to change her name and her sex and take a new start in the world."

This improbable yarn intrigued me as much as it had Mark Twain. I spent an afternoon researching it in the Cape Town library. It turned out that Mark Twain had "told the truth mainly," but not all the truth. By sheer chance I happened upon a yellowed clipping from the *Cape Times* of 1910, written by E. Rogers, Lieutenant-Colonel.

It may sound like a paradox, but we very much doubt if ever there was a woman with a past of so pronounced a type as that of the late Dr. James Barry, M.D., Inspector-General of Hospitals, who, having personated a man during her adult lifetime, died at the ripe age of seventy-one years in Down Street, Piccadilly, London, on July 15, 1865, and was then and there found to be of the female sex.

Reference to "Hart's Army List," January 1, 1865, will show that James Barry, M.D., entered Her Majesty's service as "hospital assistant," July 5, 1813, and as she was promoted to be assistant-surgeon December 7, 1815, the possibility but not the probability is that she served in the medical department of our Army at Waterloo! At all events, she was in the Crimea, yet no record of the lady's war service is placed to her credit.

It is a curious but undeniable fact that she could almost, if not altogether, choose her own foreign stations. She could be, and was, as insubordinate as she liked, without remonstrance. In a word, she was treated by the authorities as if she were—as she was—a woman.

Need we wonder, then, that her promotion was rapid, and that she even managed to jump up two steps at a time in her ambitious climb to the top. Thus she never was a surgeon, but she became sur-

geon-major November 22, 1827. She never was assistant inspector, nor brevet deputy inspector general, which were grades in the medical officers'
promotion in those days; but she became deputy
inspector-general, and then inspector-general December 7, 1858. Dr. Barry died July 15, 1865, and
her grave in Kensal Green bears the very simple
inscription, Dr. James Barry, Inspector-General of
Army Hospitals; died July 15, 1865; aged 71 years;
may still be found at Kensal Green Cemetery (Grave
19,301).

An inquest was held (in consequence of her
refusal to be medically attended in her last illness),
and next day it was officially reported to the War
Office that the deceased Inspector-General of Hospitals was in truth a woman ... Not only that, but it
was evident that in early life she had been a mother.

In 1857 I travelled with this remarkable
character on board the inter-Colonial steamer ply-
ing between St. Thomas and Barbadoes, when I
occupied the same cabin, I in the top and she in the
lower berth, of course without any suspicion of her
sex on my part. I well remember how, in harsh and
peevish voice, she ordered me out of the cabin while
she dressed in the morning. "Now, then, youngster,
clear out of my cabin while I dress," she would say.

A goat was on board to provide her with milk.
She was a strict vegetarian, nor did she take wine or
any other liquor. She was accompanied by a negro
servant and a little dog called Psyche. The doctor
was going at the time to visit her old friend and
enemy, General Sir Josias Cleote, with whom she
had fought a duel, and was wounded in the leg. ...

In person James Barry was short in stature,
angular in figure, with a long Ciceronian nose,
prominent cheek-bones and a rather lugubrious
expression of countenance. ... Imperious in manner
and officially dictatorial, in social circles Dr. Barry
was admired and respected; she was moreover,
sympathetic, and skillful in her profession.

In the Cape Town library I also found a book titled
The Fabulous People, in which David Porter gives this
information:

SOUTH AFRICA'S TIDE IS COMING IN

In 1808, when she was sixteen, she was accepted as a student in Edinburgh University, under the name of James Barry. According to the testimony of fellow-students, no one had apparently suspected James Barry to be other than she appeared. James was somewhat nervous at going through certain rough neighbourhoods at night ... and absolutely refused to box, and she had an odd manner of keeping her arms folded over her chest that the other students found quite amusing.

She served in Quebec, the Mediterranean, the West Indies and South Africa, and was once particularly commended for "assiduity and skill during a smallpox epidemic." At the Cape, she was something of a medical pioneer. In her post as Inspector of the Colonial Medical Board, she strongly opposed the prevailing practice of allowing anyone who wished to set up as a chemist and dispense medicines and drugs. She insisted that every chemist pass an examination. ... Records show that Dr. Barry devoted a lot of attention to the lepers.

Investigation after Dr. Barry's death, indicated that neither her servants nor her comrades-at-arms, despite close daily fellowship, had had an inkling of the truth. The facts about her origin were either never uncovered by the British Army or were hushed up through high-level intervention. British feminists have adopted Dr. Barry as one of their heroes [heroines].

Morning clouds had flung a white cloth over the top of Table Mountain. We took an early bus south from the city along the shoreline of the Atlantic, to see the cape itself. The drive wound along the jagged coast past holiday beaches, resort hotels, and fishing villages, and past the rugged, treeless coastal mountains called The Twelve Apostles. We counted them. The ultimate tip, Cape Point, is populated by troops of baboons and flocks of ostriches. Monuments commemorate Diaz and Da Gama, and mark where the "post office stones" received mail from early sailing vessels with warnings or advice to travellers, or messages to be delivered west to Europe or east to the Spice Islands.

AFTER YOU, MARK TWAIN

Finally we stood on a windy promontory overlooking the meeting of the Atlantic and Indian oceans. The water churned at the mixing of the cold Benguela current from the Antarctic and the warm Mozambique current from the east. Over the ocean to the west, some four thousand miles away, lay the tip of South America, Cape Horn, and the Straits of Magellan. Five thousand miles beyond that was New Zealand, then Australia. Australia was closer if we looked east, across the Indian Ocean.

The water changed from blue-black close inshore to ever-lightening shades of pearly gray until finally both sea and sky merged into silver nothingness. I had a sense, here, of the closing of the great circle of the world. I was satisfied. We could go home now.

On our last night in Cape Town, Angelika invited us to a concert of African music by a group called Amapondo. Held at the beautiful Baxter concert hall at the University of Cape Town, it proved a fitting climax to our African adventure. Our Afrikaans hostess commented as we left the house, "You'll just hear a lot of pounding." She was right. But what pounding!

It was black Africa's music—drums, drums, drums; bells, horns, whistles, wooden xylophones—strange instruments, strange musicians, strange tribal shouts, songs, and rituals. Colorful, disturbing, entertaining, funny, melodic—enchanting! It was a whale of a performance. We brought home a tape. To play it is to be transported back to that magnificent theater, to come under the spell of those compelling black musicians.

At the airport I bought an extravagant bouquet of proteas, South Africa's national flower, for our daughter in Germany. We headed north and west toward Europe remembering the overwhelming kindness and hospitality we had received in South Africa. Today we watch the news. We worry about that country. We worry about its people. We wish them well—all of them. It was good to be welcomed by children and grandchildren, and by Swedish and German relatives who had gathered to greet us after our long journey.

"We sailed on the 15th of July. ... A good and restful voyage for tired people," wrote Mark Twain. "I seemed to have been lecturing for a thousand years, though it was only a twelvemonth. ... It seemed a fine and large thing to

have accomplished—the circumnavigation of this great globe in that little time, and I was privately proud of it."

We returned home to Montana on April 3, also proud of our thirty-five thousand air miles, completely circling the globe—although less tired than Twain was. Archival research doesn't take it out of you the way lecturing does, and we had been travelling only four months. It was dark. At the far end of Flathead Lake we could see the lights of Polson thirty-five miles away.

In the morning I dug out my old bluejeans and sweatshirt and "tramped" with the dog to the top of the mountain behind our house.

I thought of elephants, jewelled women in saris, stomping African dancers, terrifying taxis. Following Mark Twain had introduced us to much that was rich and exotic—and sometimes alarming. Australia's Road of Remembrance marched through my mind; I saw again Sri Lanka's bougainvillea-festooned huts and South Africa's toiling gold miners and weaver birds.

It was spring. The sagebrush buttercups were blooming. The Mission Mountains gleamed white along the continental divide, bordering more than two million acres of roadless wilderness. The quiet of the undisturbed land, the freshness of the unbreathed air, washed by winter, seemed like a new creation after four months of summer, following the equator.

APPENDIX

Get Up and Go

Start early. This is our advice to anyone contemplating a round-the-world trip like our After You, Mark Twain expedition. Everything takes longer than you imagine it will. This was particularly true for us, living in isolated western Montana.

Expired passports were the first hurdle. We presented our old passports at the local post office, secured the needed forms, and reminded ourselves that the longest journey in the world begins with one step. Then we had passport photos made, with two dozen extras for the visas we would need for admission to almost every country we wanted to visit. Most countries require two photos.

We decided early that we needed a travel agent knowledgeable in booking beyond normal tourist routes. We had lived in Massachusetts and, after some debate and exploration, we settled on a Boston agency accustomed to scheduling Harvard and MIT scholars and consultants in and out of developing countries. We needed all the help and expertise we could get to make our arrangements.

AFTER YOU, MARK TWAIN

Airplane travel to the old British colonies does not fit into any packaged tour or the round-the-world bargain flights of any airline or combination of airlines. We flew on seventeen different carriers on our thirty-five-thousand-mile trip. It costs lots more money to choose your own route to out-of-the-way destinations. Our flights were economy class most of the way, but we were grateful that our travel agent advised us to fly business class on long ones. This was well worth the extra money for six-foot, four-inch Winston. An intermediate class, between first class and economy, it has wider seats, more leg and elbow room, and pleasant service.

A major role that a travel agency can perform is in

MARK TWAIN AND FRIENDS ON THE GO

securing visas, which were required for every country but New Zealand and West Germany—Fiji, Australia, Thailand, Bangladesh, India, Sri Lanka, the Seychelles, and South Africa. (Visas are no longer required for Fiji.) Visa correspondence and hassle is well left to a travel agent. Once again, the traveller is reminded that this takes time. Our visas for India didn't arrive until the day before our departure. State Department literature notes that one month must be allowed to secure an Indian visa. Passports must be submitted in order to obtain visas, and travel agencies have couriers who can hand-deliver passports and carry them from embassy to embassy in Washington, D.C., or to consulates in major cities.

Immunizations and health precautions also need early consideration. Under the international health regulations adopted by the World Health Organization, a country may require certificates of vaccination against yellow fever and cholera—immunizations not commonly available in the United States. Altogether we were vaccinated or got booster shots for polio, diptheria, tetanus, typhoid, yellow fever, and cholera.

In South Africa our courier for Kruger National Park insisted that we take chloroquine orally to protect us against malaria. This should be started a week before entering a malarial area and we should have been taking it throughout the Indian subcontinent. Since the last case of smallpox was reported in 1977, no vaccination for this is needed. For diarrhea, the best advice in Asia and Africa remains that of the Peace Corps: "If you can't cook it, peel it, or boil it, forget it." Then take along a handful of oral rehydration therapy (ORT) sachets, available in pharmacies, in case you get it anyhow.

With the above preventatives, natural good health, and common sense, the two of us had not a single day of illness during our entire trip. Since we were out for pleasure we made a point of resting when we were tired. It's our belief that exhaustion can generate illness. Relax, anticipate good health, and enjoy your trip. But should you get sick, here's what an experienced traveller told us: "Go to the nearest comfortable hotel, and stay there until you recover." English-speaking doctors can be located through American consular offices or hotels.

All travellers have heard horror stories of stolen passports, money, and valuables, of lost luggage, anti-Americanism, terrorism, and rudeness. We experienced none of the above. But for peace of mind and security, Winston carried several large-denomination American bills in a good quality money belt. Passports, visas, credit cards were carried in a secret pouch strapped underneath his shirt and placed under his pillow at night. These are available in most luggage stores.

All forms of ostentation should be eschewed. Our only jewelry was our wedding rings. We substituted cheap digital wristwatches for our regular timepieces. Why worry about losing valuable possessions better left at home? Although we met hundreds of people on our journey, we weren't trying to impress any of them.

When it comes to clothes—simplify, simplify. Be decently clothed, but make comfort your first consideration. Even tropical countries are sometimes cold. Take lightweight long underwear, a London Fog type raincoat, a silk turtleneck, comfortable sandals, and running shoes. My standard wardrobe is a navy wraparound skirt and slacks, drip-dry fabric. Winston favors khaki-colored slacks and shirts with buttons for access to his secret pouch. A sport jacket and dress slacks, shirt and tie saw him through. A sheath dress, sweater, and pair of pumps were my formal wear.

We each had a lightweight suitcase with wheels, sturdy, soft-sided, and as waterproof as possible. Often we had to carry these. Pack a foldable nylon totebag big enough for necessities for overnight or a weekend, or for shopping.

Our American Express and Visa credit cards were accepted at almost every hotel and gift shop. Travellers' checks were always accepted as well. We picked up mail at American Express offices in major cities. A good supply of one-dollar bills, say twenty, should be carried; these prove handy when arriving at airports and finding foreign exchange offices closed. Taxi drivers will almost always accept U.S. dollars, and there are other times when these are useful as well. When we arrive at a foreign airport, Winston waits for the luggage while I find the exchange kiosk and get enough local currency for the taxi, meals, newspapers, and incidentals for a day or two.

Travellers seem to be nervous about not being booked into a hotel when arriving in a foreign city. To avoid the sameness of large tourist hotels, we elected to stay at decent inns patronized by local people. As we journeyed, we made a habit of talking to fellow travellers and businesspeople and asking for their recommendations. We not only met many interesting travellers this way, but also saved a great deal of money. Without exception the hotels were comfortable, clean, and perfectly adequate for our use. We never were refused a room. An additional advantage is that hotels for the locals are usually more centrally located than luxury tourist hotels, and are often within walking distance of business and cultural centers.

We eat, and enjoy, whatever local people favor. The same goes for drinks. Be prepared to drink tea in any land colonized by the British. It's good tea. The coffee is uniformly awful. If you're a committed coffee drinker, bring a plastic container of your favorite instant. Boiling water is usually available in your room or down the hall. Standard procedure for us when leaving a country was to pick up a bottle of bourbon apiece at the duty-free shop. This should prove sufficient for pre-meal cocktails and nightcaps, and is a must in India where spirits are customarily not available.

The easiest place to find mementos and gifts of native arts and crafts is in government-sponsored stores in major cities. Cottage Industries in New Delhi, for instance, has a large assortment of authentic items collected from all over India at fixed prices. (They can also be relied on to package and deliver merchandise to your home.) You may be able to find treasures by bargaining in bazaars—a memorable, if time-consuming experience—but most travellers don't have the energy or expertise for such adventures. Don't depend on a taxi driver to take you to these stores. Frequently drivers will deliver you to the business of a friend, where they collect a fee and percentage of your purchases.

Don't forget a small, disposable flashlight apiece. Electricity does go off in developing countries.

For our purposes, we found the *Lonely Planet* series of travel books the most helpful. Usually subtitled "A Travel Survival Kit," they are written for both serious and lighthearted travellers. Originally they were the province of the backpacking young, but we see no reason why youth should have all the fun. These books also have good shopping suggestions and listings of local events.

I wrote to the Washington, D.C., embassy of every country we planned to visit, explaining the purpose of our journey, and asking for whatever materials or advice they could give me. I heard from all of them and received travel brochures, maps, and helpful information. A letter from the Indian embassy, presented at an airport, helped us arrange a stopover, which was ordinarily not possible in India.

Most helpful of all is a positive, friendly demeanor.

GET UP AND GO

Whenever we sought help or advice, it was quickly forthcoming. We were never threatened in any way. We were never afraid. Be adventurous. Get up and go!

And remember what Mark Twain told the reporter in Portland, Oregon, at the very start of his journey: "What's the use of making a business of travelling when you are out for pleasure?"